D0875495

# THE STRONGEST PART OF THE FAMILY

# IMMIGRANT COMMUNITIES & ETHNIC MINORITIES IN THE UNITED STATES & CANADA: No. 17

ISSN 0749-5951

## Series Editor: Robert J. Theodoratus
### Department of Anthropology, Colorado State University

1. James G. Chadney. *The Sikhs of Vancouver.* 1984
2. Paul Driben. *We Are Metis: The Ethnography of a Halfbreed Community in Northern Alberta.* 1985
3. A. Michael Colfer. *Morality, Kindred, and Ethnic Boundary: A Study of the Oregon Old Believers.* 1985
4. Nanciellen Davis. *Ethnicity and Ethnic Group Persistance in an Acadian Village in Maritime Canada.* 1985
5. Juli Ellen Skansie. *Death Is for All: Death and Death-Related Beliefs of Rural Spanish-Americans.* 1985
6. Robert Mark Kamen. *Growing Up Hasidic: Education and Socialization in the Bobover Hasidic Community.* 1985
7. Liucija Baskauskas. *An Urban Enclave: Lithuanian Refugees in Los Angeles.* 1985
8. Manuel Alers-Montalvo. *The Puerto Rican Migrants of New York City.* 1985
9. Wayne Wheeler. *An Analysis of Social Change in a Swedish-Immigrant Community: The Case of Lindsborg, Kansas.* 1986
10. Edwin B. Almirol. *Ethnic Identity and Social Negotiation: A Study of a Filipino Community in California.* 1985
11. Stanford Neil Gerber. *Russkoya Celo: The Ethnography of a Russian-American Community.* 1985
12. Peter Paul Jonitis. *The Acculturation of the Lithuanians of Chester, Pennsylvania.* 1986
19. Mary G. Harris. *Cholas: Latino Girls and Gangs.* 1988.
22. Bruce LaBrock. *The Sikhs of Northern California, 1904–1975: A Socio–Historical Study.* 1988
30. Bernard Wong. *Patronage, Brokerage, Entrepreneurship and the Chinese Community of New York.* 1988

# THE STRONGEST PART
# OF THE FAMILY

## A Study of Lao Refugee
## Women in Columbus, Ohio

Karen L. S. Muir

**AMS PRESS**
**New York**

**Library of Congress Catalog-in-Publication Data**

Muir, Karen L. S.
  The strongest part of the family.

  (Immigrant communities & ethnic minorities in the
United States & Canada ; 17)
  Bibliography: p.
  Includes index.
  1. Women, Laos (Tai people)—Ohio—Columbus—Social
conditions.. 2. Laos (Tai people)—Ohio—Columbus
—Social conditions. 3. Refugees, Political—Ohio—
Columbus. 4.Columbus (Ohio)—Social conditions.
I. Title. II. Series.
F499.C79L276  1988            305.4'889591            87–45782
ISBN 0-404-19427-3

AMS PRESS
56 East 13th Street
New York, N.Y. 10003, U.S.A.


Manufactured in the United States of America

TABLE OF CONTENTS

LIST OF TABLES

vii

# LIST OF MAPS

# ACKNOWLEDGEMENT

It is difficult to write an acknowledgement for this work—not because there is little to acknowledge, but because there is so much. There is no way to prioritize the debts that I owe to so many for the completion of this task so the following list is in no particular order. I owe much to my advisor, Dr. Ojo Arewa, who has counseled me as an advisor and a friend since my undergraduate days at Ohio State University. His advice has been indispensible. Dr. Amy Zaharlick has also given advice, counsel and friendship and it is she who first suggested the idea of my working with the local Lao community. She has not only served as a member of my reading committee, but also served as my employer on the grant she received which provided partial financial aid for my research. Dr. Erika Bourguignon has offered direction particularly in terms of the literature review and her work on the anthropology of women has influenced me greatly. Thanks also are due to Dr. Donald Bateman who served as Graduate School Representative for my oral defense. Anna Bellisari offered needed technical advice on nonparametric statistics.

The research could never have begun, let alone been completed, without the cooperation of the Lao community and the aid of my friend, Bounthanh Phommasathit. The community willingly shared its time, memories and concerns (as well as its celebrations and activities) with me for over a year and this is a great debt indeed. I thoroughly enjoyed the time I spent in the company of the Lao. Bounthanh, her husband Bounthone, and their sons Ne and No introduced me to their community; instructed me in appropriate behavior and in the Lao language; and shared their time with me. When my determination flagged, Thanh would encourage and support me. She always found time for my work as well as her own. This woman is a very special person and I cherish her friendship.

Last, but certainly not least, I must thank my family. My children were very patient with a mother who was not always available when they wanted her and proved to be wonderful ambassadors who enjoyed the time they spent with Lao friends. Similarly, my husband was patient and supportive, attending events when he was tired from his own work and putting in extra duty as babysitter, cook and housekeeper. He also drew the maps used in this work and spent endless hours proofreading typed copy. My parents gave me more than their share of time watching grandchildren and serving as a message and coordinating center.

To all of the above-mentioned people I owe a tremendous debt. I hope this acknowledgement will be accepted as partial payment. All errors and inaccuracies are, of course, my own responsibility.

# CHAPTER ONE

## INTRODUCTION

Columbus is one of ten major reception centers in the United States for various Southeast Asian refugee groups. The Vietnamese, Cambodians, Laotians and other nationalities, while sharing some cultural and linguistic features, are distinct groups, and these larger groups are made up of smaller ethnic subgroups.. These people do not perceive themselves as "Southeast Asians" (as Americans do) but, focusing on the cultural differences, regard themselves as Khmer (Cambodian), Lao, H'mong (hill tribe in Northern Laos), or Vietnamese. There are also intra-group and inter-group differences and similarities in their mutual passage through the refugee experience. Their camp experiences and the resettlement process have put stress on their traditional cultures. Some similarities in behavior may result from similarity of stress.

The Laotian community in Columbus numbers between four hundred and six hundred individuals — the exact population is hard to quantify due to the movement of families in and out of the Columbus area. This population estimate was arrived at by compiling information from various sponsoring

1

Volunteer Agencies (VOLAGS) in the Columbus area and also by an independent population assessment by Lao community leaders. The Lowland Lao form the greater part of the Columbus Laotian community and the group studied here. There are only a few families of H'mong (the highland group from Laos) in the Columbus area.

The Laotian group is the second largest Southeast Asian refugee group in Columbus. The Cambodian group numbers around seven hundred and fifty to eight hundred people and the Vietnamese group is significantly smaller numbering around two hundred to three hundred. The Vietnamese have been in Columbus for the longest period, having started resettlement in Columbus around 1976. The Lao arrived second with first members relocating around 1978; many families came in 1980 or 1981. The Cambodians began arriving in 1979 and now form the largest group of current immigrants -- probably due in part to the sponsorship of Cambodian families by the successful Cambodian Mutual Assistance Association.[1]

Most Lao refugees in Columbus were involved in an acute refugee movement. That is, they left after the communist takeover of Laos, frequently fleeing on a moment's notice with little or no possessions. Many left from "seminars" or because they were called to "seminars". "Seminar" is the word used to denote both death camps and labor camps or re-education (retraining) programs in Laos under the

communist regime. When looking at the random sample of
the local Lao community which was interviewed, one sees
that the Columbus community has members in stages of resettlement varying from early resettlement through adjustment
and acculturation (Stein, 1980). Most have been in the
United States for two to three years. It is too early to
really talk about residual changes as a result of resettlement
in this group at this time as Stein relegates the category
of residual change to the period of resettlement after ten
years or more. A few members of the local community are
approaching this period of time.

The Lao in Columbus come from a tradition of uxori-parentilocal residence (i.e. residence with the wife's parents)
and most practiced this pattern of residence before leaving
Laos. They were members of what Keyes (1975) calls uxori-
parentilocal extended families with separate but dependent
households (i.e. one household consists of parents and unmarried
sons and daughters surrounded by the households of married
daughters and their families). They also practiced or expected
to practice female ultimogeniture (inheritance of the home
by the youngest daughter) a majority of the time.

The purpose of this study is twofold. First an attempt
has been made to gather general ethnographic and demographic
information on the Lao refugee population in Columbus.
Secondly, the study focused on the women in this group,
on the adjustments they have made to life in this city,

and on the roles they play. Laotian women traditionally
have been responsible for the well-being of the family by
meeting its members' emotional and physical needs. This
idea was expressed in the Hoskins article (1976) and the
Lao community by both male and female members. The same
sentiments are echoed for Burmese women in Spiro (1977)
on Burma. In the Columbus Lao community, however, women
seem frequently to be the most insulated against external
influences: most women speak no English and have only second-
hand contact with the larger Columbus community -- contact
via husbands who work or children who attend school. Even
in families where both the husband and wife are unemployed,
it is usually the husband who will serve as the contact
with social service agencies. How, then, do these women
fulfill their roles? Are they still the "strongest part
of the family" (a phrase used by Hoskins, 1976, and by the
key informant for this study)? If not, what is their new
role? How do they fulfill their roles in the presence of
newly established needs and the destruction (due to the
refugee experience) of many traditional resources?

The proposed topic is of considerable importance for
a variety of reasons, first of all, there is a great need
for research to be done on refugees at all points of the
refugee experience (e.g. in the camps, during initial resettlement, after "self-sufficiency"[2], etc.). Information
on a particular refugee group is not only pertinent to the

group being studied, but to the refugees and the refugee experience in general.[3] In the face of the increasing number of refugees coming to the United States and the likelihood that, given the current world political situation, these numbers will continue to increase, refugee research should have a high priority. The information gathered can be of use not only to public policy makers[4] and social service/social health agencies[5], but to the refugee communities themselves. Much of the research has focused upon questions of refugee utilization of assistance programs or obstacles to providing services such as health care to refugees. These administrative problems are indeed important. Equally important is the dissemination of information about the refugee group to the larger host community in which they reside. This opens channels of communication and, it may be hoped, establishes bridges of understanding. In addition, the refugee communities can profit from the innovations and strategies of their fellow refugees in `coping with their shared experiences as refugees.

Another point of value of the proposed topic is its focus and emphasis on the role of women. There is a need for more research on the women's view of and role in a culture rather than concentration solely on the men's perspectives. In the group studied, women are particularly inaccessible to outsiders due to the language barrier and traditional cultural rules which make men the most likely contacts between

Lao and non—Lao[6]. Work in related cultures[7] has suggested that to understand the structure of these particular cultures one must understand the role of women. The present reseach indicated that this is also true for the Lao. It is particularly important, then, to observe and describe women's roles and lifestyles in these communities. Of special importance is the consideration of what is adaptive (or non-adaptive) in the strategies that are being used for daily living.

Although some may consider this study to be an example of "anthropology at home", the author does not. The research setting is, indeed, the hometown of the researcher, but the culture of the group studied certainly bears little semblance to that of the researcher who is neither a refugee, nor Lao. Because of this, the issues raised about the comparative advantages and disadvantages of "insider research" (Messerschmidt, 1981) will not be discussed here. The advantages and disadvantages specific to this study may be summarized, however. The major research advantage of the local setting was the familiarity and contacts which the researcher could sometimes utilize to assist the Lao group with programs they were considering and information they were seeking. For example, at one point a group of Lao was interested in establishing a communal garden and wanted to find out who owned a particular plot of land. The researcher was able to obtain the information quickly by contacting an old friend who worked in the appropriate department of state government. Because the researcher was established locally she was able to refer individuals to local people who could provide services or entrance into educational opportunities. The researcher was used as a reference on several applications (loan, job, or for volunteer work). In addition, she could reciprocate the extensive hospitality offered by the Lao -- at least in some small measure -- by giving children access to a local swimming pool and giving parties. The major disadvantage revolved around the same aspects -- the occasionally unrealistic expectations the Lao had of the researchers' ability to facilitate or expedite requests or proposed ideas. The locating of a large space that had cheap rental and allowed alcoholic beverages for use for the New Year's celebration proved beyond the re- searcher's expertise. The solution was to collaborate with the Cambodians that particular year, an uneasy compromise.

A further point of importance in understanding the research product is the mode of production -- specifically the interrelationship between the data, the group studied, and the researcher. As Van Esterik (1982) states

> an ethnographer is never a neutral observer, and any writing that infers neutrality is a distortion of reality. Claiming neutrality does have the function of masking the investigator's bias, and relieving him or her of the responsibility of making explicit the experiences which have colored the observations. I was not, nor am I now a neutral observer of these women.                          (p.60)

The Lao community, rather than other Southeast Asian communities, was chosen primarily because this community seemed eager to be studied. This eagerness may, in part, be due to the Lao perception of themselves as "forgotten refugees" (locally). The Vietnamese community has been in Columbus longer and is better established and better educated than the Lao refugee community. The H'mong have been targets of many United States government programs due to their close involvement with the United States troops in the Vietnamese war. The local Cambodian group is headed by a Khmer woman who is married to an American politician and has received numerous grants. In any case, the Lao have been pleased to have interest shown in them, have seemed to enjoy the visits and interviews, and certainly have made the researcher feel welcome -- above and beyond the hospitality required by their culture. Various factors made the initial contact and subsequent relationship, professional and personal, between the researcher and the key informant/interpreter very pleasant. Both the researcher and Visa[8], the key informant/interpreter, are women and there is a similarity in age (particularly important in a society where age and sex are status determinants). In addition, both share many roles and aspirations. Both had a commitment to seeing the project completed and to personal goals such as maintaining jobs without neglecting family, friends, or community obligations. This has not always been easy and it was fortunate that Visa was so tremendously supportive of the study and the researcher.

Many of the researcher's roles fit well with the community expectations for adult Lao women -- specifically wife and mother. These roles were extremely obvious due to the researcher's five month pregnant physique (or lack thereof) at the beginning of the study and the subsequent infant son who accompanied her during the research from the age of two weeks until the research was completed. Ross, the baby, proved to be an invaluable assistant in research. The researcher's older children, being at ages which are more distracting and require more supervision, did not accompany the researcher as frequently, although they did manage to make some good friends. The baby, however, was a great stress minimizer -- babies are loved by all Lao, young, old, male, and female. Whenever the researcher and son would enter a house, an older child would whisk the baby away to be admired and entertained. The women also played with him as the interview or visit progressed. Breastfeeding is common in Laos, but the women generally feel that Americans do not approve of it, preferring to bottle feed instead. It came as a pleasant surprise when the researcher would breastfeed the baby. The researcher got used to hearing pleased, but surprised expressions of *"kin nam me"* when she started to breast feed the baby. This happened frequently as interviews were conducted in the evening and the baby would get tired and fuss a little. To the Lao a fussy baby is a hungry baby and Visa would always say "maybe he's hungry" and hand him to be fed. The baby's presence not only contributed to the relaxed atmosphere of the interactions, but served as a stimulus for information regarding childbirth and childrearing. Maloof (1981) mentions a similar situation with her baby.

The researcher also carefully attempted to observe Lao custom in terms of appropriate greetings and nonverbal communication. The Lao are accustomed to accommodating Americans who, the Lao realize, think many Lao customs (such as sitting on the floor or eating on floor mats) are strange. In order to short-circuit accommodation attempts and to show respect for the Lao customs, the researcher attempted to initiate a more traditional interactive pattern. In addition, the researcher wished to minimize formality which the Lao tended to extend to her initially as a function of higher status due to educational background. By attempting to set an informal interaction, with the researcher taking more of the role of friend and showing appropriate respect to older Lao, the researcher hoped to counteract this to some extent. She seated herself on the floor at the onset of an interview and, if she needed to walk somewhere, bent over in respect when crossing in front of an adult. The researcher graciously accepted all food that was offered -- most of which was delicious! Even the fact that the researcher had long, dark hair seemed to be an advantage. The women would tell the researcher that she looked like a Lao and spent a lot of time fixing her hair in various ways. When working around the house the Lao women with long hair wear it confined in some way. When going out on important occasions, the hair is worn down and long, pulled back on either side of the face with barrettes or coiled and braided on top of the head. Most women have kept their hair long. A few of them, mostly younger women, have adopted shorter American styles. Non—offensive dress was observed, which means (for adult females) discreetly keeping the lower limbs covered with a skirt or long pants — never shorts.

Frequently tantalizing bits of information were offered that intrigued the researcher, but as all subjects can not be explored within the limitations of one study, the researcher had to leave them for a later time. As is true for all research, there are many unexplored byways that beg for further study and it is hoped that the author will be able to explore some of these in the future. Plans are currently being made to continue study on children's play and folklore within the community.

This research also involved a study of a specific instance of acculturation. Acculturation may be defined as

culture change that is initiated by the conjunction of two or more autonomous cultural systems . . . cultural changes induced by contacts between ethnic

enclaves and their encompassing societies would
be definable as acculturation . . .
(Social Science Research Council Seminar,1954,
p.976)

As such, it is necessary to present the nature of this particular contact situation[9].

Columbus is a large, midwestern city. Its population
(per the 1980 census) is 564,871 with 81% being white and
19% being non-white. There are a number of blue collar
workers (the city has 973 manufacturing establishments),
but it is primarily service and finance oriented. Being
the state capital, many people are employed in civil service
or clerical positions. In addition, eleven clearing house
banks are located here and fifty insurance companies locate
home offices in Columbus. It is also the site of the Ohio
State University, one of the big ten universities. In addition,
Columbus offers eleven other colleges or universities and
four business or technical schools. Most of the workforce
is white-collar and service oriented and many are employed
in educational functions.

There is a great deal of cultural homogeneity in Columbus.
It is a midwestern city that still retains an interest in
and an association with its agricultural roots. People
from other urban centers joke about the farm products advertised
on the major television channels. It is predominantly protestant and participates in the Puritan value system: work
is the way to success. Religion is a fairly important component
in many people's lives as evidenced by the successful effort

of religious groups to block a gay rights ordinance in city council and to retain a policy providing for the teaching of creationism along with evolution in science courses in the public schools. There are small ethnic enclaves such as West Virginians in west Columbus and small groups of Italians, Greeks, and Germans, and the Ohio State University provides some cultural diversity; but the city does not evidence the cosmopolitan, multi—ethnic ambience of many cities of similar size.

Now one can examine the nature of the boundary—maintaining mechanisms involved, These are

> the techniques and ideologies by means of which a system limits participation in the culture to a well—recognized in—group . . . (they) appear to include the relative presence or absence of devices by which the knowledge of customs and values is restricted to in—group members and thus shielded from alien influence
> (Social Science Research Council Seminar, 1954, p.976)

The United States is relatively "open" as it has admitted diverse immigrants for many years —— although the true degree of admittance has varied for different groups of immigrants. Columbus, with its high degree of ethnic homogeneity is, perhaps, more closed than other areas of the country. The Lao system seemed relatively open, in spite of its homo—geneity. The country of Laos has included several different cultural traditions and tolerates substantial geographic variability. The Lao, as an integrated part of this national culture, do not seem particularly protective of their customs.

The emphasis on respect for personal preference in Lao culture also indicates an open system. The only features indicative of a closed system are the designation of contact handlers (people who serve as intermediaries between the enclave and its host society), and a high valuation of the Lao language. Ostensibly, a high valuation is also given to the English language, but for adults this is only lip service. It is highly valued for children however.

In terms of flexibility and rigidity, the Lao must be seen as slightly on the flexible side of the middle range. The Social Science Research Council (1954) distinguishes "flexible" systems from "rigid" systems along the following lines:

> multiple or single avenues to prestige or other goals, ambiguous versus clearly defined inter-personal relationships, authoritarian versus equalitarian social controls, ascribed versus achieved statuses, prescribed versus situationally defined activities, specified versus alternative patterns of conduct, and so forth. The acme of tight integration, on the social side at least, is probably achieved in systems which sanction autocratic powers in one or a few elite roles, such as absolute monarchies, theocracies, and gerontocracies
> (p 976)

Greenbaum (1973) follows the same lines when characterizing societies as flexible or rigid. Rigidity is evidenced by nonegalitarian, ascriptive status; autocratic hierarchical political systems; fixed residence and restricted travel; centrally controlled, fixed religious rites; and fixed group membership with changes permitted only by higher authority. Flexibility is evidenced by egalitarian, achievement-oriented status; federated or stateless democratic society; freedom of travel and ease in residence changes; individual control over flexible religious rites; and freedom to join a variety of diverse groups. Laos, in a real sense, was a nation of federated, relatively independent provinces. Avenues to prestige are not singular, nor are they multitudinous. They consist of a combination of ascribed and achieved statuses. For example, one avenue of prestige, i.e. temple life, is available only to males (see Van Esterik, 1982). Another prestige factor involves family of birth (hereditary leaders), also ascribed. Yet there are alternate avenues of prestige such as being a good householder, or a teacher. Prestige may be obtained via achieved factors such as wealth, or education. Flexibility is reflected in the situational orientation of Lao interaction which chooses among prescribed alternatives. One may treat a relative as a friend as well; and a friend as a relative. The fact that alternate patterns of conduct are always present and that interpersonal relationships must be considered "ambiguous" (Social Science Research Council Seminar, 1954:976) rather than clearly-defined are also indicators of flexibility. The researcher does not agree with characterizations of Lao social relations as lacking structure however10.

Lao culture seems fairly efficient in terms of self-correcting mechanisms. These allow "the cultural organism to shift function and to adapt internally" (Social Science

Research Council Seminar, 1954:977). There is a definite degree of permissiveness in individual role performance. Only monks attempt to live by all the precepts of Buddhism all the time. Others are only expected to conform in varying degrees. One excellent example of a self—correcting mechanism can be seen in religious influences within Laos. One must remember that each attempt to regain balance may also alter the social base upon which that balance is poised. In other words, the cultural base line may change over time and still be considered self—correcting. The basic spiritual beliefs of the Lao in *phi* (spirits) has survived, in a modified form, the influx of Buddhism and Christianity. The new religious systems have been incorporated into the old, in part through the process of compartmentalization. That is, one can be Buddhist and still, on a personal level, seek aid from the *phi*.

In ecological respects, acculturation is taking place in an environment which is directly disruptive to the major traditional subsistence pattern of the Lao. That is they can no longer farm (*het na*). Acculturation has "set new limits on the possible relationships of man and nature" (Social Science Research Council, 1954:979). The contact situation has also disrupted social relationships —— due to the refugee experience —— but a viable community does exist within the Lao group in Columbus. There is a sufficient number of individuals of various ages and sexes to form a community and no real imbalance in sex or age distribution has been created. Likewise, contact has been with a balanced host community, in terms of age and sex. The close, daily contact has been preponderantly with lower income groups, but is somewhat balanced by more infrequent and formal contacts with the middle class. Exposure to mass media (in the form of television) might also mitigate any imbalance -- albeit while creating its own inaccuracies and biases.

# CHAPTER TWO

## PREDECESSORS

There are several excellent general works on Southeast
Asia. Osborne (1979) presents an historical overview for
the area which summarizes briefly information for each specific
country. Kundstadler's (1967) book <u>Southeast Asian Tribes</u>,
<u>Minorities, and Nations</u> presents extensive historical and
ethnographic information on the area in general. Burling's
(1965) book is a classic work on Southeast Asia and deals
with the similarities and differences between various Southeast
Asian groups. There is little literature specifically on
Laos. Burling states that the best summary work on Laos
itself is the HRAF Press book on Southeast Asia by LeBar,
Hickey and Musgrave (1964) -- this author concurs. The
LeBar and Suddard book (1967) is a more detailed, updated
version of this work focusing exclusively on Laos. It contains
a wealth of basic ethnographic material dealing with geography,
history, religion, social structure and the economy. The
only possible shortcoming is an unavoidable one — it is
written before the communist takeover and so does not encompass
the time span or effects of this change.

Many contemporary works emphasize the highland group
(the H'mong) rather than the lowland Lao. The H'mong had
heavy involvement with the United States during the Vietnamese
war period and so were well known to many westerners. In
addition, they are very different from other Laotian groups
because they are members of hill tribes who still practice
hunting and gathering, shamanism, and farm opium as a profitable
cash crop. In contrast the Lao are basically rural subsistence
farmers involved in a major world religion — Buddhism.
Hardly as striking a contrast, and so perhaps the Lao seemed
less interesting to western scholars.

There are several books which treat specific aspects
of Laos; for example: politics and government (Halpern,
1965); its relationship with the United States (Stevenson,
1972, and Halpern and Halpern, 1964); and traditional medicine
(Halpern, 1963). The Indochinese Mental Health Project
(1980) in Minneapolis, Minnesota has also compiled a brief
summary highlighting the traditional cultural similarities
and differences between the four major groups of Indochinese
refugees: Vietnamese, Cambodian, H'mong and Lao. This summary
provides information on major customs and topics such as
childbirth practices, wedding rites, and funerals. It is
useful as a guide for those who find themselves unexpectedly
dealing with Southeast Asian refugees (e.g. health care
providers or teachers) and in the fact that it separates
and calls attention to the distinctions between the various

ethnic groups. Chaplier and Van Malderghem (1971) present a brief, but useful description of life under Pathet Lao administration that illustrates the conditions prevalent when most of the Columbus refugees left their homeland.

A fair amount of literature deals with the Vietnamese war period and its effect on Laos. Most useful are those by Adams and McCoy (1970); Burchett (1970); Branfman (1972); and Fall (1969). A highly personal account is found in Marek Thee's book (1973) Notes of a Witness: Laos and the Second IndoChina War.

Examples of literature dealing specifically with traditional aspects of H'mong culture include Cooper (1978, 1979) on spirit ceremonies; Gua (1975) on cultural ecology; and Westermeyer (1971, 1974) on the use of drugs and alcohol.

Although the present study deals with the Lao in a non-traditional setting, it is hoped it will illustrate some aspects of traditional Lao culture and so to help fill this gap in information.

Research on Lao women seems, at this point, to be minimal. Several works do suggest starting points for research, though. The three most significant are Potter's (1977) work on the structural significance of women in a Northern Thai village; Hoskins (1976) article on Vietnamese women and their role options; and Van Esterik's (1982) book on Southeast Asian Women. It should be noted at this point that there is a great deal of genetic, cultural and linguistic similarity

between some Thai and the lowland Lao.  For this reason
research on Thai groups may apply, at least in some respects,
to the Lao.  Historically much of Thailand has been traded
back and forth between the two countries -- as the interpreter
for this study explained it:

> You cannot trust Thai men.  They are always fighting
> and they lie to you.  They only want to get ahead.
> Long ago 16 provinces of Thailand were part of
> Laos.  The Thai men had a big dinner and invited
> the Lao leaders.  They fed them dinner, then they
> killed them.  Now those places are part of Thailand.

While the researcher could not substantiate this particular
incident, the people and the land have undoubtedly changed
hands many times (LeBar and Suddard, 1967).  In the Van
Esterik (1982) book on Southeast Asian Women, nothing deals
specifically with the Lao, but particularly relevent to
present concerns are the introduction (which covers the
status of women and the state of women's studies in Southeast
Asia); Kirsch's (1982) article on women in Thailand (which
deals with the definition of sex roles in terms of Buddhism
and a changing economy); and Van Esterik's (1982) article
on laywomen and their roles in Therauada Buddhism (which
is the variety of Buddhism practiced in Laos).  Van Esterik
also raises the question of exactly what the assumed "high
status" of women in Southeast Asia really represents — a
matter addressed specifically in Chapter Five of this study.

Potter's (1977) work deals with the idea that the "loose
structure" attributed to the social organization of Thai
society (Mosel, 1966; Phillips, 1965) is not, in fact, loose.

It is instead organized along affinal rather than consanguineal ties. Specifically, inheritance goes from father to son—in—law and residence is largely uxori—parentilocal (i.e. with the wife's parents). Upon marriage, the man not only changes residence, but also pays respect to his wife's ancestral cults. These affinal ties then become major integrating ties of the community. Phillips (1965) defines the family in terms of a nuclear family structure, although only 30% of the families in the community Phillips studied conform to this ideal. He says there are no rules for living arrange- ments, yet his descriptions reveal a tendency for men to live with their wife's family after marriage. Phillips' study may be somewhat less appropriate to extensions to the Lao community in any case as it deals with a group that differs somewhat ecologically (being in an area that is more isolated) and culturally (e.g. linguistically) from the Lao of Laos. The people of northern Thailand differ from the people of southeast Thailand and Laos. Ingersoll (1975), dealing with a more northeastern Thai group disputes Phillips' claims, suggesting that the community Ingersoll studied is indeed communally based and has no doubts as to their identity. Phillips' (1965) portrayed the community he studied as individualistic, nonconforming and unstable. Keyes, in support of Potter's findings, also suggests that researchers have overemphasized the role of descent in attempting to analyze Thai structure and thinks that residence is a more important factor.

Spiro (1977) in <u>Kinship</u> <u>and</u> <u>Marriage</u> <u>in</u> <u>Burma</u> presents a picture similar in many aspects to traditional Laos. Parallels exist in use of personal choice in selecting a mate (much more frequent than arranged marriages); in the ideas about ideal characteristics for spouses and in many ideas about male superiority and dominance (which is founded in Buddhism). In spite of these ideas of male dominance, in both Burma and Laos the woman exercises much control because of her traditional familial and economic roles.

Hoskins (1976) article attempts to illustrate that the roles and employment chosen by Vietnamese women in a modernizing society are not incongruent with their traditional roles as many Westerners seem to feel. They are, in reality, consonant with the basic traditional roles in their functions — specifically in providing for their families and in controlling family finances.

This current study attempts to address the above mentioned concerns: the structural status and cultural status of Lao women and their changing roles as they face a modernized society.

There is a great deal of literature on refugees and immigration. Much of it is of somewhat limited utility to the current research because the immigrants were economically well-off and well-educated — most of the local Lao community

are rural farmers with little formal education. The cultural
and physical differences between host and refugee also are
more diverse for this group then for many previous groups.
Much of the refugee research, to this date, has been piece-
meal. It has been generated as overworked agencies struggle
to cope with overwhelming numbers of refugees in everyday
situations. Various publications by the Indochina Refugee
Action Center (1979, 1980a and 1980b) summarize the statistics
on refugees and organizations involved in the resettlement
problem. Liu's work (1979), although on Vietnamese refugees,
is a keystone work for all refugee research, summarizing
the refugee experience and illustrating the dilemnas with
which refugees must come to terms in starting a new life.
Volume 55, number 3 of Anthropological Quarterly is devoted
entirely to Southeast Asian refugees in the United States.
Most articles deal with public policy (Howell, 1982; Orbach
and Beckwith, 1982; and Haines, 1982) or aspects of communities
that impinge upon social service agencies (Dunnigan, 1982;
Scott, Jr., 1982; and Finnan, 1982). The only ethnic groups
dealt with specifically are the H'mong and the Vietnamese.
Works on mental health and health problems are also fairly
prevalent (e.g. Academy for Contemporary Problems, 1979;
and Muecke, 1983). General works on Laotian refugees (although
of limited use being short, magazine articles) are Kales'
(1970) and Garrett's (1974) articles in National Geographic.
This dearth of research on Lao refugees, as opposed to the

H'mong of Laos, is one good argument for the need for this study as the two groups differ greatly, both culturally and in terms of experiences in the refugee process. Refugee research has been "sporadic, unsystematic, isolated, and cursory" (Stein, 1980:1). The seeming diversity of refugee experience is somewhat superficial. Stein (1980) summarized this idea well:

> the basic premise . . . is that there is a refugee experience and that this experience produces what we can call refugee behavior. (p. 1)

With this premise in mind, one can place individual refugee and refugee group experiences into a continuum of refugee behavior. Several models provide useful concepts and approaches. Keller (1975) has defined the stages of refugee experience as: threat perception; deciding to flee; the flight with its concomitant danger; reaching safety; camp behavior; repatriation, settlement, or resettlement; early and late stages of resettlement; adjustment and accul- turation; and residual states and changes in behavior caused by the refugee experience.

One must also keep in mind that which distinguishes refugees from other immigrants. Bernard (1976) presents an article that delineates the differences and similarities between immigrants and refugees — as much useful for separating these two groups theoretically as for the information it contains. Kunz (1973) makes the following useful distinction: immigrants are _pulled_ to their new lands by expected opportunity. Refugees, on the other hand, are <u>pushed</u> out of their homeland. Refugees did not want to leave; if they could stay in their homeland they would, and if they could return to it, most would do so immediately. This is a theme that is reiterated over and over again in the interviews conducted for this study. Kunz (1973) identifies two basic types of refugee movements: the anticipatory refugee movement (before crisis) and the acute refugee movement (after the crisis has occurred). Anticipatory movements allow more preparation for departure and more transportation of goods. Another important concept from Kunz's work is the idea of "vintages" or associative groups of refugees who leave a country, frequently in waves, as the political climate undergoes change. In the case of the Lao, the earliest wave included higher military officials and individuals who worked with the Americans. Later waves were mostly rural people who were dissatisfied with the communist way of life. There is a problem fitting the Lao into some theoretical models. Newman (1973) distinguishes between voluntary migration and forced migration. The Lao fit neither category comfort—ably. They were not brought to America by force, yet they did not necessarily choose to come specifically to America. They were at the mercy of the camp authorities as to their final destination, but they left their homeland on their own.

One can identify specific characteristics associated
with refugees, particularly acute refugee movement participants.
These are guilt (for leaving loved ones or inability to
save loved ones); invulnerability (the idea that refugees
are survivors and have been through the worst already);
and aggressiveness (probably a function of the other two).

Similarly, prolonged camp experiences may make refugees
more apathetic and dependent than they were before camp
experiences (Murphy, 1955, Stein, 1980). Stages have been
proposed to deal with the resettlement process, breaking
it down into certain time spans characterized by specific
pyschological outlooks (Stein, 1980). During initial resettlement

> . . . the refugee will be confronted by the reality
> of what has been lost. From a high occupational
> and social status at home they will plunge downward
> in their new land. From professional to menial,
> from elite to an impoverished minority. And they
> will confront the loss of their culture -- their
> identity, their habits . . . Strains will appear
> at home because the husband can't provide, the
> women must work, the children don't respect the
> old ways, and, because they acquire the new culture
> more rapidly, the children socialize the parents.
> Nostalgia, depression, anxiety, guilt, anger,
> frustration are so severe that many refugees toy
> with the idea of going home even though they fear
> the consequences . . .                          (p 16)

After the first year and one half or so

> . . . is the drive of the refugees to recover
> what has been lost, to rebuild their lives . . . they
> will work hard and try many new approaches to
> rebuild their lives . . . many will change jobs,
> go to school, and move from their initial placement
> to an area of refugee concentration. They will
> also experience increased problems within the

> family, and the level of mental dysfunction is
> likely to shift and increase.                    (p 17)

Late stages of acculturation are characterized as follows:

> After four or five years the refugees have completed
> the major part of their adjustment. The dream
> . . . conflicts with reality.  The refugee has
> acquired the language and the culture, been retrained,
> worked hard.  If the goal is not near, or at hand
> now, the refugee is likely to abandon the efforts
> . . . drive and determination wane, discouragement
> sets in . . . many refugees talk of their exodus
> as having been for the sake of the children; hopes
> are transferred to the next generation.     (p 17)

The final outcome occurs after ten years or more.

> . . . the refugee group will have achieved a certain
> stability.  The sum total . . . is one of decline.
> Despite the drive and determination, the effect
> of exodus is to produce lower status.       (p 18)

One might ask what constitutes a "successful resettle-

ment".  Stein (1980) suggests three different sets of criteria.

The government judges success by reduction in numbers of

refugees utilizing public assistance programs and by increases

in refugee employment.  Volunteer agencies tend to judge

success by a reduction in the number of "refugee problems,

demands, and complaints" (Stein, 1980:6).  Both of these

can be misleading because they may measure a shift in dependency

from American to refugee resources and are negative: "out

of sight, no problem" (Stein, 1980:7).  The last criteria

would be that of the refugees who seek to obtain a quality

of life that approximates or surpasses that of their old

life. For most, this is romantic and unrealistic. Operational-

ly speaking one might judge success for Lao families or

individuals on the basis of self-sufficiency of basic needs

— including those of hospitality and patronage. One may rely on community resources in order to fill basic needs, but only in traditionally accepted patterns such as patronage (as opposed to charity). An attempt to apply this model to the local Lao community requires a time span beyond the present scope of research, but is something to be addressed in the future.

The question of assimilation may be dealt with by using Gordon's (1964) idea of three models which confront refugees upon arrival in a new culture: host conformity; the Melting Pot (merging of host and refugee — a highly romantic idea); or cultural pluralism. Most Lao refugees in Columbus have chosen the third model. This means that the refugee will go with the dominant pattern when involved in outside contacts such as politics, education and employment, but will preserve his/her communal life and culture within his/her home and social sphere. This being the case, research on women is a major key to reaching an understanding of what is happening as women are associated with many of the aspects of Lao culture that are maintained. Gordon sees Eisenstadt's (1954) first three stages of acculturation as behavioral assimilation (learning the language, norms, customs; learning to perform new roles; and formation of new values about oneself) and as compatible with cultural pluralism. The fourth stage, however, is structural rather than behavioral and involves entrance into host institutions. The eventual outcome of

this stage, according to Gordon (1964), would take generations
and result in host conformity instead.   Boone (1981) points
out that urban immigrants with relatively high levels of
education and occupational training use ethnic maintenance
to combat the isolation and disintegration which can occur
in American suburbs.   This ethnic maintenance provides an
"identity" at will.   For many reasons, this fourth stage
of host conformity may not be achieved.   For example, physical
differences such as those possessed by the Southeast Asians
(darker complexion, oriental features) may impede host conformity.   Stein (1980) points out that these new refugees:

> are culturally and ethnically vastly different
> from their hosts . . . and they have a different
> attitude toward being a refugee; because many
> see themselves as temporary exiles who expect
> to return home, they reject assimilation
> (page 24)

Newman (1973) points out that attempts to enter the system
of the host country often leads to an increased awareness
of peoplehood and unity due to the need to organize -- this,
in turn, may lead to rejection of assimilation in the next
generation.   Newman proposes that alternating emphasis on
assimilative and pluralistic goals with succeeding generations
may be the norm rather than an anomaly.   Van Amersfoort (1982)
on a study of Dutch immigration distinguishes racial minorities
(those physically distinguishable from the majority) from
ethnic minorities (only culturally distinguishable) and
cites racial minorities as more enduring.

The present study will attempt to judge the utility of some of the various models in assessing the refugee experience for the local Lao community.

It is important to note that in an urban setting the "ethnic community" may not be geographically localized.

> In these cases, communities may develop "patterns" of communications through which they maintain their identity:  networks based upon kinship and personal friendship; and various types of voluntary associations . . . which provide the means for frequent contact between community members
> (Maloof 1981:70)

In these cases it is not common residence that establishes an ethnic enclave but

> common memories, a common language, common values, and numerous "cultural interests" (e.g. literature, arts, food, and festivals) form the "content" of their interaction.  The economic and political events of the "old country" are also foci of interest and concern.
> (Maloof, 1981:70)

In order to maintain the community and its "life blood" (Maloof, 1981:71) people maintain contact using the telephone and visits facilitated by automobiles.  All of these descriptions apply to the Columbus Lao community as well.  The "ethnic community" is not geographically localized, although there are geographic centers; common cultural interests provide the ethnic bond; and closeness is maintained through telephone visits as well as physical visits.  The car is indispensible and almost every Lao household in Columbus owns one.  These topics are addressed in more depth in later chapters.

In addition Haines, Rutherford, and Thomas (1981b) make some points relevant to the present study in their paper on Vietnamese refugees in Washington, D.C.  There are three major points to be addressed.  First, refugee adjustment is a process mediated by social groups and is not simply a transformation of the individual per se.  Individuals may be the significant social unit, as among the Vietnamese, with respect to ideology or action.  This would also be the case with the Lao, at least ideally.

> But the individual is defined by, and acts in reference to, a structure of relationships.  Each set of relationships is associated with distinctive obligations and expectations . . . we see the refugee . . . as a person inextricably embedded in a complex social network which is, itself, to be considered a resource in the resettlement process.  The importance of community and extended family among refugees has been amply noted . . . the internal community structure, and specific rights and obligations associated with family and community, have not been explored as fully.
> (Haines, Rutherford, and Thomas, 1981b:96-97)

The present work is designed to expand on precisely this area of information and focuses on commitments between family members, friends and community members and, particularly, on women's networks.

Secondly, American analytic domains such as family versus community or economic versus kinship, are frequently deceptive in refugee studies.  Certainly they would be so in the current study where these domains clearly overlap.

Thirdly, the adjustment process cannot be understood without attention to its extent through time, including

the process of secondary migration. The author argues this
same point when suggesting that one great need is to continue
to study this community as the acculturative process continues.

The major study on the Lao as refugees is Van Esterik's
(1983) report. It differs from the present study in several
ways. Firstly the Lao Van Esterik studied lived in three
different counties and were a much smaller group than the
Lao community in Columbus. Van Esterik also is investigating
networks, but focuses primarily on the male, political,
patron-client relationships and ensuing networks rather
than on the female networks. Lastly, Van Esterik's major
goal is to assess use of various refugee programs by the
Lao and policy implications arising from traditional Lao
culture and male networks. In many ways Van Esterik's study
may be seen as the flip side of the coin to this study:
his focus is predominantly on male organization and the
interaction of the community with external programs while
this author's is predominantly on female organization and
internal relationships of the community.

## Methodology

One purpose of this project is to create an ethnography
-- that is, a description of the way of life of the Lao
refugee women in Columbus and of their adaptive strategies
for daily living in particular. The construction of an
ethnography involves specific methods of data collection

and the use of certain basic approaches or values. These
values are those that are central to all of cultural anthropology 1) an attempt to understand the emic or insider's
perspective of the culture; 2) the idea that the interrelationships of various aspects must be considered so that the
larger picture is accurately described (i.e. the whole is
greater than the sum of its parts) -- or the holistic approach;
3) that data must be dealt with in context rather than in
isolation -- or contextual analysis; and 4) the idea of
cultural relativism -- or the avoidance of application of
value judgements to the group studied (rather considering
the group's customs as problem solving strategies involving
problems common, in some form, to all cultures.)1

The specific data collection techniques used included
participant observation. In this case, actual residence
was not set up with the group involved, but data collection
involved a combination of observation and participation
in both daily routine and in special events. Boone (1981)
mentions that urban anthropology differs from more traditional
anthropology in

> requiring a great deal of telephone work, the
> driving of long distances, and the extension of
> the scheduled interview into an opportunity for
> participant observation                    (p 57)

The researcher of this study concurs. In addition both
Boone (1981) and Bennett(1981) mention the obligations involved
in doing fieldwork on literate, academically expert immigrants.
Many of the Lao leaders fall into this group. This situation

requires self-examination on the part of the anthropologist
as to objectivity, and the opportunity for feedback from
the community. The researcher plans to make the dissertation
available to those members of the community who are interested
in reading it.

In addition, use was made of key informants for further
elucidation of specialized fields of knowledge (e.g. religious
ceremonies) and as contact persons who supplied much of
the initial information regarding the culture.

Some data were collected through formal, open-ended
interviews which touched on various aspects of life. These
aspects included demographic information; background histories;
future plans; ideas about children; attitudes toward education;
and linguistic information, among others. The interviews
were administered to fifty families (approximately 50% of
the local Lao community) with the aid of two interpreters.
Visa served as the main interpreter, but her husband did
interpret on eight occasions when she was not available.
The selection of the families to be interviewed was randomized
(although an attempt was made to interview families in different
parts of the city, as there are several clusters of Lao
population), participation was voluntary, and interviewees
could elect not to answer specific questions (none ever
did). A gift of thanks ($5.00) was given to each family
interviewed. The money was given to the male head of the
household if he was present and was then given by him to

the female head of the household or to one of the children. Traditionally extra money may be given to children to spend as they wish. If the male head of the household was absent, it was given to the female head. The interviews took place in the respondents' homes and both interpreters were well known, well—liked members of the community2. No tape recorder was used as this practice seemed somewhat disturbing and distracting to the respondents.

More casual, informal interviews were conducted as opportunity arose (e.g. during preparation for parties, during visits, or during planning sessions for community festivals).

By combining data obtained by these various methods, one potentially has access not only to the ideal cultural patterns (or what people say one should do), but also to the real cultural patterns (what people actually do).

Initial contact with the Lao community in Columbus was established by the researcher in June, 1982. The researcher went on a home visitation trip with Yvonne Jones of the Columbus Public School System and Dr. Amy Zaharlick of the Ohio State University. The visit was to thank parents for allowing their children to participate in a teachers' workshop on multicultural education. The workshop was given by Dr. Virginia Allen of the Ohio State Universiy earlier in the summer.

After contacting Mr. Thong, who frequently serves as an interpreter and contact for the community, the researcher was referred to Visa as an excellent female interpreter who might be able to help with the research.3  A meeting was arranged and the researcher subsequently began attending a variety of functions (e.g. birthday parties, mutual assistance activities, Mutual Assistance Association meetings, an American New Year's party, etc) within the community.  Visa served as an interpreter and explained the researcher's interest in the Lao community and in Lao women.

Dr. Zaharlick received a grant from The Center for Urban Studies at the Ohio State University and subsequently employed the researcher as an assistant to conduct the fifty formal interviews of the families and paid for the use of any interpreter for this specific function.  Dr. Zaharlick's study involves the production of general demographic and historical information on the various Southeast Asian groups in Columbus.  The interview used in this study combined questions of a general nature pertinent to the above mentioned goals and more specific questions dealing with this researcher's goals.  This study may be seen as a more detailed, in-depth illustration, concentrating on the Lao, of the general outline to be produced by Dr. Zaharlick's study.  The researcher continued to participate in other activities, visiting families, going shopping, going fishing and having picnics while conducting the interviews.  In a sense, data collection has never really ended as the researcher still maintains contact with the Lao community. Artifically one might designate January, 1984 as the end of the fieldwork as contact since that time has been less frequent.

The cultural description itself was generated by seeking patterns of behavior and their interrelationships. An attempt was made to describe in some basic fashion the history and backgrounds of the Lao in Columbus; the present coping strategies employed by the women; and general information on the Lao culture in its new American setting and the feelings of the Lao toward their present circumstances. It was difficult to deal effectively with the question of retention of traditional patterns and with future plans of the refugees due to the apparent problem the Lao had in dealing with counterfactual questions included in the interviews. For example, when asked "what would you tell someone coming here that would help them learn how to live in Columbus", the respondent would commonly answer "I do not know anyone coming here." The uncertainty of their present economic situation also placed restraints upon future planning. One could look no further, with certainty, than the public assistance benefits lasted.

# CHAPTER THREE

## THE NEW ADDITION -- Vital Statistics

The following data is derived from the fifty formal interviews conducted by the researcher. Although one interview may involve more than one family living at the same address, the employment data and life history information apply only to the focal family at a particular address. That is, the couple (or individual) who are seen as senior and so in charge of the household are considered the focal individuals. An interview list was picked from a roster of local Lao families compiled from volunteer agencies and the community. A random sample was selected from each geographic area where the Lao live in proportions representative of the size of the Lao refugee population in that particular area. The familial status of the individuals included in the interviews is shown in Table 1. The terms "single males" and "single females" are misleading in a sense, since no one in the community lives alone. Females away from parents tend to be better integrated into the household than do single males who are considered independent and free to come and go at will. Most single males in this group were living with "uncles" or "cousins"[1] and the youngest single male was thirteen years old. This boy was living with his sister, her husband, and their family. He had taken the husband's last name so that the man could claim him as a dependent and so bring him to the United States with the family. Some single males also live with same age friends who are married. The single female group included one divorced female who, with her young daughter, was living with her uncle and his family. The other two cases both involved an unmarried younger sister living with the older, married sister's family.

TABLE 1

Familial Status of Individuals Interviewed

| | | |
|---|---|---|
| adult (parents with children)[a] | | 106 |
| 2 parent | 50 | (100 individuals) |
| female head of household | 2 | |
| grandfather | 1 | |
| grandmother | 3 | |
| single males[b] | | 16 |
| single females[c] | | 4 |
| dependent children[a] | | 156 |
| total number of individuals | | 282 |

[a]married individuals, regardless of age, are considered as adult rather than children. Likewise, single males and females residing with parents are considered children regardless of age.

[b]males living with household other than parents, regardless of age.

[c]females living with household other than parents, regardless of age.

The adult category includes two cases of a mother living with her married daughter's family; one case of a mother living with her unmarried daughters and her grandson whose father, her son, and mother were still in Laos; one case of parents living with a married daughter's family; and three sets of parents living with unmarried children having married daughter(s) and family living nearby. The uxori-parentilocal extended family tradition has been maintained in these cases.

Table 2 shows location of birth for those individuals classified as children. Table 3 gives a breakdown of persons in the child category by age and sex.

Table 4 shows the village/town of orientation for focal individuals in the interviews (i.e. the parents of the focal family). The village/town of orientation is the one in which a person spent the majority of his/her time under the age of twelve. This designation is necessary as many

TABLE 2

Interviewed Children's Place of Birth

| | |
|---|---|
| Laos | 117 |
| Thai refugee camps | 11 |
| Philippine camps | 3 |
| United States | 24 |
| Ireland | 1 |

TABLE 3

Interviewed Children (by Age and Sex)

|  | Male | Female |
|---|---|---|
| 5 and under | 36 | 27 |
| 6 to 10 years | 24 | 21 |
| 11 to 15 years | 19 | 15 |
| over 15 years | 11 | 3 |
| total | 90 | 66 |

individuals moved around a great deal and may have spent very little time in the village of birth. Town designations, rather than specific villages, are used since respondents seemed to orient toward a particular town as a center for activities (markets, visiting, ceremonies, etc.). See Map 1 for locations of these villages/towns. In addition, one individual was born in China and another, in Thailand.

TABLE 4

Village/Town of Orientation for Adults

Northern
| Xieng Khouang | 7 |
| Vientienne | 26 |
| Paksane | 2 |
| Samneua | 5 |

Middle
| Thakhek | 5 |
| Savannakhet | 15 |

Southern
| Khong Sedone | 16 |
| Pakse | 9 |
| Champassak | 12 |
| Sithadone | 2 |

MAP 1

Village/Town of Orientation
and Thai Refugee Camps for Interviewed Adults

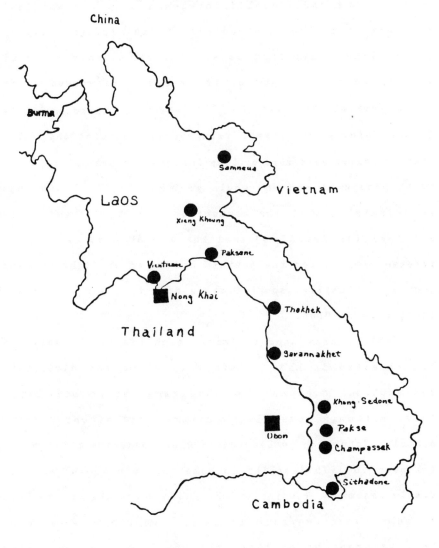

Movement between China and northern areas, and Thailand and southern areas of Laos seems to have always been rather common. One individual interviewed actually was living and working in Thailand and went to the refugee camp from there rather than from Laos. Another couple followed a similar route. Twenty of the males interviewed and two of the females spent time in "fighting back" camps in Thailand before joining the formal refugee camp populations. These fighting camps were more or less informal efforts at organizing small groups of men who would go back into Laos and engage in skirmishes with the communists. In these cases, wives and families usually joined the men at Ubon or Nong Khai refugee camps after the husband had tired of fighting camps. Twenty-two families spent time in Nong Khai and twenty-eight spent time in Ubon.

Table 5 shows the training which the focal individuals had received in Laos. This only shows the distribution for adults. Most children had received no schooling in Laos, although some older children had attended primary school. Schooling in Laos was disrupted during the communist takeover in 1975 (earlier in some northern areas) and never really resumed. Ten individuals worked for the United States in some capacity while in Laos. Two others were related to government or military personnel and, as seen above, thirty individuals actually worked as soldiers, police or government workers. It is interesting to note that males

TABLE 5

Previous Training in Laos for Interviewed Adults[a]

| training | | number of individuals |
|---|---|---|
| **Male** | | |
| less than completion of primary school | | 13 |
| 0 years | 5 | |
| completed 3rd grade | 5 | |
| completed 5th grade | 3 | |
| finished primary school | | 33 |
| soldier, police, or government training[b] | | 30 |
| temple training[b,c] | | 4 |
| attended or completed secondary school | | 13 |
| attended university | | 1 |
| **Female** | | |
| less than completion of primary school | | 34 |
| 0 years | 17 | |
| 1 year | 1 | |
| 3 years | 6 | |
| 4 years | 9 | |
| 5 years | 1 | |
| finished primary school | | 17 |
| nursing training[b] | | 5 |
| formal sewing training[b] | | 3 |
| typing[b] | | 1 |
| attended or completed secondary school | | 3 |
| attended university | | 1 |

[a]areas overlap: e.g. soldiers may also have completed primary school, etc.

[b]this training does not require other formal education, not even primary school.

[c]individuals in this category spent a longer time than the time ritually required of males in this culture in the temple.

referred to grades completed in school, without talking about years spent, while females talked about years spent in school without reference to the grades completed. Perhaps level of education is a more important factor for males than females. That is, males tended to concentrate on the grade achieved since level of education is a factor effecting status for males. Females tended to concentrate only on the time spent in school since education is not an important factor in their status determination. Their status derives more from that of their husband (or father) and having a great deal of education might even make it difficult to find a man who is superior in education and so, an appropriate mate. Those women who did pursue specialized training,

TABLE 6

Languages for Interviewed Adults
(not including English learned in the United States)

| | Male | | Female | |
|---|---|---|---|---|
| | Speaking Only | Literacy | Speaking Only | Literacy |
| 1st Language | | | | |
| Lao | 10 | 43 | 24 | 29 |
| Thai | | | | 1 |
| Chinese | | | 2 | |
| Vietnamese | | | | 2 |
| 2nd Language | | | | |
| Lao | | | 1 | 3 |
| Thai | 15 | 20 | 22 | 11 |
| French | 2 | 3 | 2 | 1 |
| Vietnamese | 1 | | | |
| Cambodian | 1 | | | |
| Chinese | 1 | | | |
| 3rd Language | | | | |
| French | 7 | 8 | 1 | 6 |
| English | 1 | 2 | | |
| Thai | | 1 | 1 | |
| 4th Language | | | | |
| English | 1 | 9 | | 3 |

centered studies on service occupations such as nursing
or teaching. Having a daughter in these positions brings
honor to families because the daughter is earning <u>bun</u> by
helping others. Most women stopped working upon marriage,
however.

It should be noted that facility in English is frequently
greater than in French even though respondents would name
French as learned before English. This is because English
was usually acquired and used in the army or on a job while
French was learned in school, rarely used, and easily forgotten. From Table 6 one can see that the majority of both
males (45%) and females (55%) are bilingual — either in
Lao and Thai, or another native language and Lao. Here
similarities between the males and females cease. 31% of
females have use of only one language; 9% control three
languages and 5% control four. For males, the percentage
of multilinguals is greater: only 20% are monolingual;
17% use three languages and 18% use four. Eighteen percent
of the males had significant exposure to English in Laos
as compared to only 5% of the women. 45% of the women are
illiterate in their first language as compared to 19% of
the men. Many of the men gained literacy while serving
in the temples as novices, even if they did not attend primary
school. Women cannot exercise that option.

Thirty eight families fall under Stein's (1980) second
stage of resettlement (expanded here from one to two years

to include one to three and one half years in the host
country).  Twelve families fall into Stein's third category
of resettlement (expanded here from four to five years to
three and one half to ten years in the host country).  No
families fall into the initial stage (up to one year in
the host country) or the ultimate stage (over ten years
in the host country).

Stein characterizes the second stage of resettlement
as follows:

> (the refugees) will work hard and try many new
> approaches to rebuild their lives . . . many will
> change jobs, go to school, and move from their
> initial placement to an area of refugee concentra-
> tion.                              (Stein, 1980, p. 16)

Indeed twenty-one of the families interviewed had been involved
in secondary migration.  One family had moved six times,
but the others had each relocated only once.  As Stein suggests,
all but one of these secondary migrations did occur within
the first two years of resettlement.  The one exception
occurred in the third year of resettlement.  Pursuit of
job opportunities, extra income opportunities (e.g. worm
digging) or desire to be near relatives, other Lao, or a
Lao community where people "really helped each other" were
frequent reasons for moving.  There is no assurance, however,
that further secondary migration will not occur in this
group as welfare benefits and other government aid becomes
unavailable locally.

Stein characterizes the third stage as:

> the dream . . . conflicts with reality. The refugee
> has acquired the language and the culture, been
> retrained, worked hard . . . drive and determination
> wane, discouragement sets in.
> (Stein, 1980, pp. 16-17)

In addition, Stein (1980) as does Murphy (1955), mentions
the apathy that is caused by lengthy stays and enforced
dependency in refugee camps. How do these models and pro-
jections fit the local Lao community?

Table 7 shows the employment status for the various
households interviewed; Table 8 shows the types of jobs
held by the refugees since coming to Columbus; and Table
9 shows the companies most frequently mentioned as employers
by the Lao interviewed. Certain employers have become
relatively good job sources for the Lao because Lao refer
out-of-work friends or relatives to them when there is an
opening and, in some cases, because the employers benefit
from the Lao's lack of activism and organization in labor
unions. The figures in Table 8 and 9 include positions
held previously even if the individual is now laid off from
the job. On the basis of Stein's (1980) suggestions one
might expect to find that refugees in the second stage of
resettlement are better off in terms of employment because
they are more actively seeking it; and more involved in
school. None of the adults interviewed were currently attending
any vocational training or other educational programs.
This leaves the question of employment status. One may

TABLE 7

Employment Status of Interviewed Households[a]

| | |
|---|---|
| no job | 23 |
| one parttime job | 4 |
| two parttime jobs | 1 |
| one parttime, one fulltime job | 2 |
| one fulltime job[b] | 13 |
| two fulltime jobs | 5 |
| more than two fulltime jobs | 2 |

[a]number of people varies; nuclear family and relatives living with them.

[b]women provide the primary source of income in four of these households.

TABLE 8

Types of Jobs Held by Interviewed Lao Refugees

| sex | job | number |
|---|---|---|
| male/female | odd jobs/maintenance/janitorial | 8 |
| female | seamstress (machine) | 13 |
| male | machine operator | 22 |
| male/female | meat grinder | 3 |
| female | government clerk | 1 |
| male | cook | 1 |
| male | material handler | 1 |
| male | auto painting | 1 |

TABLE 9

Most Frequent Employers of Interviewed Lao

| Company | number of males | number of females | total number of Lao |
|---|---|---|---|
| Columbus Steel Drum | 10 | -- | 10 |
| Betlin | 5 | 3 | 8 |
| Colemco | 1 | 5 | 6 |
| Capitol Manufacturing | 3 | -- | 3 |
| G & M Machine Products | 3 | -- | 3 |
| Capitol City Poultry | 1 | 2 | 3 |

propose the following null hypothesis:   there will be no
significant difference in the employment status of refugees
in the second stage of resettlement when compared with those
in the third stage of resettlement.   The alternative hypothesis
states that there will be a significant difference.   The
data is summarized in Table 10.

TABLE 10

Employment Status as Related to
Stage in Refugee Resettlement

| household<br>employment status | Stage II<br>refugees | Stage III<br>refugees |
|---|---|---|
| no job | 18 | 5 |
| less than one fulltime job | 4 | 1 |
| one fulltime job | 9 | 4 |
| more than one fulltime job | 8 | 1 |

Using the Kolmogorov-Smirnov Two Sample Test (Frank, 1976),
which examines differences between two samples, one finds
that the $D$ (Kolmogorov-Smirnov statistic) value is 0.114.
This value is much lower than the critical value of $D$ (at
0.01 level) which is 0.556.   Accordingly one must accept
the null hypothesis:   there is no significant difference
between the two groups in terms of employment.

Table 11 shows employment status by sex for the focal
individuals interviewed.   Using the Kolmogorov-Smirnov Two
Sample Test, one finds that $D$ is 0.2534, below the critical
value (at 0.01 level) of 0.3310.   There is no significant
difference between males and females in terms of employment
status either.

TABLE 11
Employment Status by Sex for Interviewed Individuals

|  | Male | Female |
|---|---|---|
| No job | 27 | 36 |
| Parttime | 1 | 5 |
| Fulltime | 20 | 8 |

One might also suggest, using Stein's (1980) model that increasing time spent in refugee camps and the apathy and dependence created might lead to decreased employment status. Length of time in refugee camps might also be seen as increasing the probability of secondary migration. One primary reason for secondary migration is to regain governmental aid and benefits. That is, when benefits run out in one city, a refugee can migrate and receive benefits again in a new city. Also different areas vary in the extent of aid offered and the amount of time eligibility is considered. If increased camp time leads to increased dependency, this dependency could well manifest itself in increased secondary migration. Table 12 shows employment data as related to

TABLE 12

Employment Status as Related to Refugee Camp Stay

| Household Employment Status | Short Camp Stay | Long Camp Stay |
|---|---|---|
| no job | 8 | 15 |
| less than one fulltime job | 2 | 3 |
| one fulltime job | 3 | 10 |
| more than one fulltime job | 4 | 5 |

a short (up to one year) stay versus long (over one year) stay in refugee camps. Table 13 shows the length of refugee camp stay as related to presence or absence of secondary migration. Again using the Kolmogorov-Smirnov Two Sample Test, one finds that $D$ for Table 12's data is 0.083, far below the critical value (at 0.01 level) of 0.487. The $D$ value for Table 13's data is 0.229 below the critical value (at 0.01 level) of 0.464.

TABLE 13

Secondary Migration and Length of Camp Stay

| Length of Camp Stay | Secondary Migration | No Secondary Migration |
|---|---|---|
| up to one year | 6 | 11 |
| one to two years | 6 | 13 |
| two to three years | 4 | 3 |
| four years and over | 5 | 3 |

In other words there is no significant difference between the lengths of camp stays for those families who participated in secondary migration and those who did not. There is also no significant difference between the employment status of those who had a short refugee camp stay and those who had longer stays. Perhaps the combination of Lao realism (LeBar and Suddard, 1967) and the plateau effect (Van Esterik, 1983) that causes the Lao to level off in effort once certain necessities are achieved have produced the results contrary to Stein's model. That is, drive and determination are not influenced by time in host country or time in refugee camps as much as by attaining life's necessities. Likewise, the length of camp stay seems to have had little effect on the Lao in terms of increased dependency on government aid and secondary migration.

One can also look at some of the characteristics of the local Lao community as revealed by those interviewed. A car is important not only to get to work, but in terms of visiting and for status. It is hardly surprising, then, that forty-two of the households had one car to use and five had two or more. Only three households had no car and one of these was an all female household where no one drove. The other two depended on cars owned by relatives who lived nearby.

The practice of marriage in Laos follows a pattern of areal endogamy. A person tends to marry someone from his/her own area -- not necessarily their own village, but from a nearby village. Table 14 shows the frequency of endogamy for marriages which occurred in Laos and marriages which occurred outside of Laos (i.e. in camps or after resettlement).

### TABLE 14

Frequency of Areal Endogamy

|  | marriage in Laos | marriage outside Laos |
|---|---|---|
| spouse from same village/town of orientation | 23 | 12 |
| spouse from different village/town of orientation | 8 | 6 |

One can see that endogamy is practiced by 75% of those who married in Laos and by 67% of those who married outside of Laos. By applying the *chi*-square test, which compares observed outcome frequencies to expected outcome frequencies, one gets a $x^2$ value of 0.3161 which is below the critical value (0.01 level) of 6.63490. This means one must accept the null hypothesis of independence of the factors of whether one marries a spouse from one's own area of Laos and whether one marries within or outside of Laos. In other words, areal endogamy continues to be practiced even beyond the confines of Laos.

A similiar analysis can be made of attitudes toward the use or nonuse of physical discipline. Categorization into groups with use or nonuse of physical discipline was based on responses to interview questions and observations. Where observation conflicted with stated norm (only two cases, both involving spanking when parents said they did not use this method), observations were considered the deciding factor. The refugee group can be divided into those who have had children for three or more years in Laos and those who have not. The reasons for choosing three years as a boundary are given below.

> 1) due to Lao cultural practices a child does not begin to function in an independent role until somewhere between the ages of two and three years.[2]

2) this is an age when ego development and assertive-
   ness frequently begin.

3) therefore this is an age where parental/child
   conflict may logically be predicted to begin
   to be experienced. At the onset of conflict,
   parents must decide upon appropriate disciplinary
   techniques and philosophy.

The author feels that if these conflicts occur within the
context of the extended family in Laos, parents would be
more likely to follow traditional, nonphysical means of
discipline[3]. Those parents who experience these initial
conflicts outside of traditional society and the guidance
of the extended family, may be more likely to use the type
of discipline frequently observed by the Lao among Americans,
physical discipline. Table 15 summarizes these data.

### TABLE 15

#### Preferred Mode of Discipline[a]

| Children for three or more years in Laos | use of physical discipline | nonuse of physical discipline |
|---|---|---|
| yes | 6 | 25 |
| no | 15 | 4 |

[a]the mode used most frequently is indicated
although any particular individual may occas-
sionally use the other mode as well.

The $x^2$ value here is 17.1732, far exceeding the critical
value (0.01 level) of 6.63490. The null hypothesis must
be rejected. There is a correlation between the two factors.
The $x^2$ test can not point to a causal relationship however.

The preceeding explanation is merely the author's offered rationale for the relationship.

A further topic of interest is the size of Lao families. For this, a division is made in the refugee group between those who were married for five or more years in Laos and those who were not. Five years was chosen because this amount of time allows traditional child-bearing attitudes to be implemented. A couple married in Laos for less than five years might have started child-bearing but would not be as firmly entrenched in traditional attitudes toward child-spacing and family size as would couples who are midway toward family completion. A simple computation of arithmetic mean shows that the average number of children for those married five years or more in Laos is five. The average for the other group is two. Some may argue, however, that this is simply a reflection of the length of time a couple has been married. This is a valid criticism and one finds that the average length of marriage for the first group is 17.6 years; for the second, 6.3 years. One might then compare a ratio -- number of children per years of marriage -- for the two groups. This is actually more a measure of child-spacing. The data for this comparison are summarized in Table 16. Using the Kolmogorov-Smirnov Two Sample Test, one finds that the $D$ value is 0.066, which is below the critical $D$ value (0.01 level) of 0.471. This means there is no significant difference in terms of child-spacing between

TABLE 16

Comparison of Number of Children per Years of Marriage

| number of children per years of marriage | married five or more years in Laos five | married less than five years in Laos |
|---|---|---|
| none — 1/5 | 2 | 2 |
| up to 2/5 | 17 | 17 |
| up to 3/5 | 3 | 4 |
| up to 4/5 | 1 | 2 |
| up to 1 | 0 | 0 |

between the two groups. This topic is a good example of the limited utility of statistics in ethnographic description. Firstly, in this particular case, there was no adequate way of accounting for miscarriages, abortions, or stillbirths among the population. Secondly, the researcher agrees that child-spacing remains the same in both groups. If one were to analyze the data again in ten years, however, the author feels confident that significant differences would be found. There is no doubt, empirically, that ideas about the ideal number of children have changed. Availability of contraceptives and abortions, and economic conditions have led to a desire for fewer children among those refugees who are still in the initial stages of family development, who have two or three children. In traditional society they might continue on to have five or six children, but almost all women told the researcher that two or three children was all that they wanted. When the husband was present he concurred with this statement. A more relevant statistic, not available

at this time, would be a comparison of the size of <u>completed</u>
family between the two groups. The families in the second
group are still having children at essentially the same
intervals but are stopping after two or three children.
Economic pressures seem to be the major concern.

The distribution of the Lao population locally (as
reflected by the families interviewed) is given in Table
17. See Map 2 for locations. Van Esterik (1983) mentions
that in the community he studied there was a division between
northern and southern refugee groups. It may be useful
to analyze local residence patterns as they relate to village
of orientation for a couple. Where this factor differs
for husband and wife, the village of the longest residence

TABLE 17

Local Distribution of Interviewed Families

| complex | number of families |
|---|---|
| East 1 | 10 |
| East 2 | 12 |
| East 3 | 3 |
| Other East[a] | 7 |
| Subsidized Housing (Metro) | 5 |
| University area | 2 |
| North | 3 |
| Westside doubles[b] | 8 |

[a]families here are not in any apartment complex.
Households are distributed on different streets
or parts of streets in doubles.

[b]these households are clustered on the same
blocks.

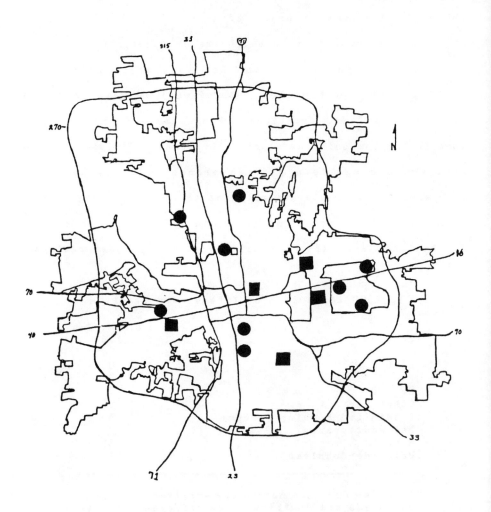

MAP 2

Local Distribution of Interviewed Families

■ -- indicates clustered residences

● -- indicates scattered residences

after marriage for the couple is used. Table 18 summarizes these data. The refugee population has been divided by (northern, middle, southern) rather than village for simplicity and only clustered residences (e.g. complexes) are analyzed.

### TABLE 18

Local Residence and Region of Previous Residence in Laos

| Region | East 1 | East 2 | East 3 | Metro | University | North | West |
|--------|--------|--------|--------|-------|------------|-------|------|
| northern | 3 | 3 | 2 | 2 | 1 | 1 | 7 |
| middle | 0 | 4 | 0 | 3 | 0 | 0 | 1 |
| southern | 7 | 5 | 2 | 0 | 1 | 2 | 1 |

From a quick perusal one can see that refugees from the middle region are concentrated in East 2 and the subsidized housing areas. One can also see that the westside location is primarily used by northern families. Southern families are clustered in the eastside complexes. Some clustering would be expected as people are frequently informed of empty apartments with low rent by relatives or friends who are generally from the same region. But is the clustering significant? By applying the *chi*-square test one finds that the $x^2$ value is 21.1198. The critical value for $x^2$ with 12 degrees of freedom is 26.2170 at the 0.01 level and 21.0261 at the 0.05 level. The results, then, show significance at the 0.05 level. At this level one must reject independence of the two factors. There is some relationship between local residence and the region of Laos from which people come. Simply by looking at the data one can also state

that most local areas have representatives from more than
one region of Laos so there is no clear-cut division between
the regional groups as suggested by Van Esterik (1983) in
the group he studied.

CHAPTER FOUR

THE NEW ADDITION - GENERAL ETHNOGRAPHIC DATA

Through the Eyes of Others

Laos is a small country, but nonetheless it contains
many regional differences. Visa said her young son once
asked her why she and his dad talked so differently -- she
laughed and told him she came from Vientienne and spoke
the right way while his dad came from the south (Khong Sedone)
where they talk funny. Laos was originally a collection
of kingdoms. Disputes between various rulers at various
times caused drastic shifts of boundaries throughout its
history[1]. At the time of French colonization (1893), there
were three major kingdoms: Luang Prabang, Xieng Khouang
and Champassak. The French selected Luang Prabang as ascendent
and demoted the other kingdoms to the status of provinces
and their kings to the status of governors. Laos became
an independent state in the French Union in 1949; and an
independent nation in 1954 (Halpern, 1960, Osborne, 1979).
In many ways it is an artificial creation of the French
since it had no previous independent existence.

Traditional Lao life is an annual routine of planting,
cultivation, and harvest (LeBar and Suddard, 1967). Most
Lao are illiterate, subsistence farmers. There is a rainy

63

season (May to October) which encompasses a busy planting
time with much village ritual, and the leisurely growing
period. This is followed by the dry season filled with
the intense activity of harvesting, threshing, winnowing
and storing the rice. Travel is only really possible during
the dry season and so activities which require travel, including
politics, are postponed until this time. The monsoon has
been predictable and so wet-rice farmers like the Lao have
a basic conservatism and satisfaction with life -- a situation
not enjoyed by the dry rice farmers of the hills. Wealthier
farmers may have buffalo or other large animals and almost
all farmers have chickens or other small animals as well
as an extensive vegetable garden.

Buddhism is in many ways the center of Lao life --
a fact reflected by the central and prominent placement
of the village wat (temple). Theravada Buddhism concentrates
on merit-making and is not terribly prohibitory for the
layman. It emphasizes individual efforts to progress or
regress and the right of an individual to choose his/her
own path. Most Lao try to embody the Buddhist virtues of
self-restraint, modesty, generosity, and serenity which
are manifested in good manners, hospitality and respect.
Self-restraint also entails a quality one might call equanimity
or the concealment of any displeasing emotion. Added to
this core of Buddhist values is the Lao value of individual
responsibility.

Most rural Lao are bound closely to their village of residence as many in the past had little information regarding the world beyond. This situation was altered by the travel many men did in military or government service during the war.

Although Laos has been subjected to many influences -- French colonialism, American aid, warfare, communism -- the traditional way of life and values have been maintained to a large extent. The larger cities had obtained many Western imports before the communist takeover -- movies, bars, clubs, postal and telephone services and newspapers -- but the rural Lao remained largely untouched. Even the urban population remains closer to the rural than might be expected, a major reason being the low level of industrial development[2].

In the 1950's the United States became involved in Laos out of concern for the spreading influence of communism in Southeast Asia. Because of this concern, the United States employed various civil servants and police who, understandably, turned to the United States for help after the communist takeover in 1975. Some of the refugees interviewed worked for the United States government or were soldiers or police officers associated with the pro-United States government. Many of the Lao refugees in Columbus came from southern Laos and from rural areas. Most attended a primary school for some time and many were fulltime farmers.[3] It was not unusual in Laos for adult males to be absent from the family for prolonged periods due to job obligations or, more recently, government service or "seminars". It was the women who were left to raise the children and tend the farm in the men's absence.

Most of the Columbus refugees are in Stein's stage two category (Stein, 1980). Actually, Stein mentions only the first two years in the host country and then jumps to the fourth and fifth years of resettlement. In this study the second stage has been expanded to take in the third year as well. Stein (1980:16) characterizes the second stage as follows:

> (the refugees) will work hard and try many new
> approaches to rebuild their lives . . . many will
> change jobs, go to school, and move from their
> initial placement to an area of refugee concentra-
> tion. They will also experience increased problems
> within the family, and the level of mental dysfunction
> is likely to shift and increase.

This stage, then is characterized by great drive and determination to regain lost status.

Secondary migration within this group has occurred for most of the local Lao population within this time period as Stein suggests. For the local population, though, it is impossible to say if the preceding migration(s) are the final migration. Many of the local Lao say that if they cannot obtain jobs in Columbus, they will go elsewhere to find jobs, or to pursue better public assistance programs. The question of restoring the refugee's old status is somewhat problematical. Most of the local male refugees did not

have any significant status in Laos -- other than the status
of being self-supporting adult males with families. Similarly
women had little status beyond that of the wife of a self-
supporting male. Only one of the women interviewed (a
nurse) continued to work after marriage. Basically, then,
the only status to be recovered is that of self-sufficiency
and cultural competence. Perhaps the refugee experience
is filtered through the traditional Lao realism[4]. In any
case, none of the families interviewed voiced any expectation
of obtaining any particular status within American society.
Some individuals were seeking to better themselves, but
the training or job was always seen as instrumental to
obtaining a traditional source of security like a house,
or in terms of boosting the status of a man within his
own community, rather than as an attempt to gain an American
status comparable to the one held in Laos. For example
a patron might obtain a job that allows him to offer a
service to prospective Lao clients -- the job does not
necessarily carry any particular status in American society
(e.g. a used car salesman or insurance agent). These individuals were also rare. The local refugees, for the most
part, were interested only in survival, basically feeling
that English and vocational training were wasted on them
(the adults). One interviewee told the researcher that
he had attended English classes several times but he had
not understood anything - "maybe I'm too old". All were

hopeful that their children might have a bright and successful future -- a shift in emphasis from self to the next generation that Stein (1980) does not project until the succeeding stage of the refugee experience.

American society appears to be somewhat Janus-like to the Lao and they are, understandably, reluctant to embrace their new host's culture whole-heartedly. There is much in the United States in terms of material wealth when compared to Laos. As many of the Lao said "everyone here has a TV and a car -- even us". Much of the old sources of security are gone, however. The Lao are impressed with American material culture and public assistance. Many of the Columbus Lao are getting their first taste of electricity and running water. Public assistance provides money for those who cannot find jobs and every family can have their TV and their car (and usually cable television channels and Atari game machines). But this bounty causes discomfort as well. Public assistance is desparately needed for food and medical attention, but most Lao expressed a dislike for taking handouts in this form. Visa explained it thus:

> It is hard for a man not to work. In Laos, nobody needs a job because you always have the farm. Your family will have food and you can live. Your family is there to help. Here you need money for everything and to get money you need a job. If you don't get a job, you get welfare. But with welfare, someone else must take care of your family and you are useless. It is hard to be useless.                    (personal conversation)

American society is seen as very restrictive in some ways. Visa's husband joked to the researcher:

> In the United States you need a license for every-
> thing:  to hunt, to fish, to pick food, to drive,
> to get married — probably to die.  If you die
> without a license, they say "no, you can't die
> yet, go stand in line and get your license first".

Americans are also seen as basically unfriendly. Many of the women complained that Americans all stay inside their houses with their doors and windows shut and that Americans never talk to their neighbors. This perplexes the Lao who are used to coming, going, and conversing freely with the whole community.

On the other hand, the Lao feel that American society is far too permissive in other respects. The most disturbing are those involving perceived disrespect and sexual mores. While admiring American society for making "everyone equal, no one is a king"[5], some expressions of equality cause discomfort. Calling an adult by the first name, without any title is very uncomfortable for the Lao. When they talk to Americans about community members they use Mr. and Mrs. as titles. One is referred to as Mrs. Visa or Mr. Thong (Mr or Mrs. plus first name of individual). One interviewee expressed disbelief that Americans just step over another's feet and walk by without showing respect or acknowledging the person's presence at all. The Lao fear greatly the lack of respect Americans have for the elderly. This same fear was expressed repeatedly: in Laos the aged are respected and cared for by their children; in America the aged are cast away and institutionalized. The researcher constantly heard adults now in their twenties or thirties express concern over growing old in this country and their fear that their children would "put them away somewhere". In addition, there is the disrespect of American youth in their general conduct, the drinking and swearing.

The Lao are mildly uncomfortable when exposed to casual public signs of affection between spouses -- and the definition of public here means wherever there are witnesses, even in one's own home with one's children present. Visa once commented that she thought it was nice for a husband to kiss his wife when he came home from work, but "we could never do it". Even greater discomfort is evidenced at the touching, kissing, and hugging displayed by American teens and Americans in general, when it crosses sex lines. Touching, hugging, and kissing as signs of affection and friendship are expected between Lao women, for example. Touching, and hugging are acceptable for Lao men as well. Several Lao commented to the researcher about Richard Dawson, a game show host who is known because he kisses all female contestants on his show. "He is so silly. He is a flirt," they would say. "He kisses everybody. Why does he do that?" Perhaps because personal control of the display of emotion is so important to Lao culture, the Lao perception of Americans is that they are excessively sexually permissive.

Several of the men told the researcher that "the Lao do not live together before they are married like all you Americans do". This view of American society is undoubtly encouraged by the viewing of soap operas and music videos on television.

Black Americans pose a particular adjustment problem for the Lao. The Lao are frequently thrown in with the blacks in low income housing. The Lao are aware of the ideal American stand on prejudice and quick to voice disclaimers against prejudice. The standard refrain heard by the researcher went "I am not prejudiced, but it seems that . . ." followed by a negative statement. Example of negative statements include "blacks get in trouble more than whites", "blacks drive too fast", "blacks rob people or hurt them". Newman (1973) outlines certain factors that influence the presence and nature of conflict between ethnic groups and several of these seem particularly appropriate to the current situation. Firstly, Newman points out that an increased perception of threat leads to an increase in conflict. That the Lao and lower income blacks are in competition for the same job pool and assistance programs -- both of which are shrinking in size -- is undeniable. Furthermore, once a company hires a Lao worker, it frequently hires more. The Lao explain this by saying that the employers tell them the Lao may not know the language, but they work hard. A more cynical person might suspect that employers are benefitting from exploitation of non-English speaking workers who do not understand how to use the labor system to their own advantage. The Lao are not organized nor activists in labor unions or labor rights movements. As the Lao regard blacks as a threat, so blacks, rightly, perceive the Lao as a threat in the labor market.

Van Esterik (1983) also suggests that blacks may feel slighted and look with askance at the train of middle class tutors and sponsors who help the refugees, but do not associate or help with the refugee's black neighbors. In reality, at least within the local community, there is very little contact, particulary at the refugee's home, between such personnel and the Lao refugees. Why, though, should suspicion be directed toward lower income blacks and not lower income whites who are in a similar relationship to the Lao economically speaking? During the course of the study many instances of friendliness were observed between the Lao and white neighbors -- although relationships were by no means overly congenial or very close on a continuing basis. Only extremely rarely did any friendly contacts take place between the Lao and their black neighbors.

Traditional Lao social structure is organized by hierarchies based on age, sex, education, and other factors. It seems that the Lao may be ordering their new host society into hierarchies as well. Despite the lip service paid to ideas of equality and lack of discrimination, Americans obviously rank whites above blacks. Whites tend to hold better economic positions and positions of power. The Lao, accepting this hierarchy, would therefore be less likely to criticize white Americans than black Americans. This does not mean that the Lao like everything about white Americans, it just means that out of respect for a higher statused group, they would not express their dislikes as freely, particularly to a member of the higher statused group. Practicality also enters the picture. It is whites who are most likely to serve as patrons (in the role of sponsor or tutor.) to the Lao and it is inherently unwise to offend potential patrons. The fact that the researcher was white may have increased this tendency to not criticize white Americans. Some indication of this effect can be seen in the fact that, during interviews, people usually distinguished between educated white Americans (favorably regarded and commented upon by the Lao) and uneducated white Americans (more neutrally treated). In casual conversation criticisms of educated white Americans were made occasionally. Most complaints involved perceptions of unfriendliness, or the feeling that the Americans look down on the Lao and regard them as stupid.

Another factor influencing conflict is the dissonance between the cultures (or subcultures if the reader prefers) of the blacks and the Lao. The ideal behavior for the Lao is to be quiet, polite, and controlled in everyday life; to show respect to people; and to speak pleasantly. Drinking is permissible (and on the rise among unemployed males who are free to drink whenever they wish instead of only when not working), but to be drunk is not well-regarded. This last prohibition does not necessarily apply to Lao parties or celebrations. The Lao's black neighbors, on the other hand, come from a culture which expects louder talk, an enjoyment of verbal conflict; and the evidencing of more exuberant behaviors in general (e.g. swearing, singing loudly, dancing, etc.). One may also appear in public drunk. The dissonance between the two cultures is destined to make the Lao feel uncomfortable.

Newman (1973) also discussed the difference in a horizontal social structure between segregated and integrated communities (in a geographical sense) in terms of the nature of conflict. In an integrated community conflict is frequent, but usually less intense or violent. In a segregated community conflict is less frequent, but more intense. The Lao and blacks are members of geographically integrated communities. Most direct complaints (i.e. based on first hand experience) by the Lao involve blacks being too noisy or saying unpleasant things to them. They say that the blacks tell them that the Lao had no right to come to the United States and take the jobs and welfare money away from the blacks. The most severe complaints are mostly second hand (i.e. based on another person's experience or a general belief of the community not based on any particular incident) and involve fear of theft or assault, perpetrated by blacks against the Lao. It is interesting to note that the actual incident involving the most violence took place between a lower income white man and a Lao family. In this incident, the man shot bullets through the windows of the Lao family's home. No one was injured, fortunately.

Newman (1973) suggests that the refugee experience may forge allies where none existed before (e.g. amongst Jews from various eastern and western European countries). There has been some cooperation between Southeast Asian groups, but mutual distrust fostered by the Indochinese conflicts does exist. A recent occurrence involved the shooting of two Vietnamese (one injured, one killed), reportedly by Lao. The two communities have explained it on the basis of actions of irresponsible young men involved in love triangles. There is some mutual conflict between members of the two groups, although the leaders of both groups are working cooperatively on refugee concerns. It is unlikely that any true alliance will occur. Newman points out that alliance is shattered if one group progresses more quickly than another. The Vietnamese in Columbus have been in the United States for a longer time and generally were better educated and from a higher social class in their home country than are the Columbus Lao. The leader of the local Cambodian group is married to an American who

is involved with local politics. For these reasons, the
local Lao already perceive themselves as far behind the
other two major Southeast Asian groups in the city. Newman
further describes geographic spacing as determined by the
dominant group in a society. The dominant group has indeed
tried to scatter the Lao, ostensibly for economic reasons
(i.e. to relieve the burden on any one city of providing
public assistance funds to the refugees). This has also
reduced any seedling organization or power within the group.
The Lao, however, have resisted this initial dispersion,
and, through secondary migration, have regrouped into geographic
clusters.

The Lao fit Newman's model of pluralistic goals alternating
with assimilative goals. The present generation of adults
is very interested in maintaining the traditional culture
and community, although it recognizes the utility of learning
to speak English and in getting skills with which to obtain
a job. The adults want their children to learn to speak
(and in some cases, to read and write) Lao and to learn
to "be Lao". This generation of adults has no interest
in assimilating into American society. The next generation
already shows signs of a shift in goals. One man told
the researcher that he told his daughter (age four years)
that she was Lao. She replied, "No, Daddy. You're Lao.
I'm American". The children all like American clothes,
music and food and many are adopting increasingly unLao-like

behaviors and manners -- calling each other names and being
similarly disrespectful. Some of the children refuse to
eat traditional food. Visa buys American food for her
older son (age seven years) because he does not like to
eat Lao food at home all the time. An occasional adult
will say they have no desire to return to the old ways,
to return to Laos, and that they are very pleased with
America. These individuals are very few, however, and
fall into one of two categories: those who left Laos at
a young age and have parents in the United States; or those
who were somewhat disenfranchised in Laos (e.g. Lao-Chinese
who suffered discrimination while in Laos). Most adult
Lao leave no doubt that they consider themselves apart
from Americans and prefer it that way. Few are interested
in citizenship in their host land and most voice a desire
(more or less wistfully, depending on their acknowledgement
of reality) to return to Laos. The fact, that these refugees
are not citizens also causes them to be uprooted (as Newman,
1973, describes migrant workers) in the sense of being
deprived of rights like the right to vote. Because of
this, they may also move, following public assistance programs.
There is no evidence of desire for assimilation. Everyone
would gather around in pleasure when the researcher brought
out a map of Laos. People would eagerly point out where
they had lived in Laos and places they had enjoyed. Almost
all the adult Lao talk about how they miss their homes,

their farms, their gardens, their friends, and the beautiful
countryside of Laos. The weather here is too cold in winter
and there is no river nearby to offer relief from the heat
in the summer. America may be the land of opportunity
and a rich, new land; but, like the humble Kansas native
surrounded by the glories of Oz (The Wizard of Oz, 1939),
the Lao refugees firmly believe "there's no place like
home".6

Status, Conflict, and Conflict Avoidance

One of the core values for the Lao community in Columbus
is respect. One shows respect in many ways: through hospitality, politeness, and the use of specific linguistic
and nonverbal markers. The way one says "yes" varies with
the status of the addressee as does the nonverbal behavior.
Among peers one would say yes "uh"; to someone who is respected,
one would say "doy". Similarly the absence or presence
of the clasped hands and bow for greeting is dependent
on status. The placement of the clasped hands varies with
the status of the addressee: chest level, the level of
the face, or the level of the forehead may be used as status
increases. Status is determined in the local community
by the same factors used in traditional Lao society (Lebar
and Suddard, 1967; Van Esterik, 1983). Relative age is
important, younger respecting older. It is interesting
to note that actual chronological age is not important,

however. Several respondents had difficulty figuring out their chronological age and several others had unofficially altered their ages for reasons of convenience. One man reduced his age by three years while in Laos in order to be able to attend the police academy. Another man added two years to his age while in the United States to be eligible for a job corps program. There is similar disregard for last names -- several refugees used the last name of someone already in the United States in order to expedite their resettlement. Minors also took names of an adult and came as his relatives for the same reason (i.e. one woman's younger sister and brother use her husband's last name). Social affiliations and networks are of primary importance and if changing one's last name will promote a favorable affiliation, it is done. Most Lao refugees have no documentation to dispute or support such claims, and none is required.

Gender is important, female respecting male. Education or religious affiliation (i.e. affiliation with a temple through priesthood or training) raises status. Ties with respected families or individuals in Laos also lead to increased status in the local Lao community. In accordance with the idea of hierarchies, the head is seen as the most respected part of the body. None, except the parents, should touch a child's head. When one crosses in front of another, the head must be lowered so that it is (symbolically, if not literally) no higher than the other's head.

An example of an extension of this was seen when Visa told the researcher that a learned Lao told them to move their bedroom when they had first come to Columbus and were living in a house provided by their sponsor. Actually it was part of a seminary and was shared with several other families. The reason given for moving was the presence of a bathroom (on the floor above) over the bedroom. This clearly violated the norms for respect to one's head and one's person. It is the greatest insult to point to or touch anything with one's foot. Everyone should be polite and in control at all times. Many parents told the researcher that they "respected" their children and that is why they only talked to them when they misbehaved, instead of punishing them.

Part of politeness which proves particularly disconcerting to Americans (and is a great potential pitfall for research) is the Lao habit of telling someone what the Lao think she/he wants to hear -- instead of what the Lao really feel. For example, Bert and Josie (pseudonyms) who are associated with a local fundamentalist church found a dish-washing job for one Lao man. He only worked for three days then stopped showing up. They asked him what was wrong. He told them the job was too hard for him because he had back problems and could not stand so long or lift heavy trays. Bert and Josie were satisfied with this explanation. At a later time, the researcher heard the man telling some Lao friends that the job only paid $3.50 an

hour and had no health care benefits and that is why he
had stopped going to work. To tell Bert and Josie the
true reason for quitting might have insulted them by implying
that their help had been unsatisfactory. Indeed Bert and
Josie may well have had difficulty understanding. Many
middle class Americans seem to feel strongly that those
on welfare should take any job over none at all. In reality
increasing one's income slightly can cost extensive public
assistance benefits and lead to a condition of net loss
for the family.

Another extension of politeness is avoidance of conflict.
Unlike middle class Americans who seem to value confrontation,
the Lao avoid it[7]. At a meeting designed to help various
public service agents better understand Southeast Asian
refugees and their problems, one American participant communi-
cated her distress at the fact that two Vietnamese families
she knew had not spoken to each other for three months.
She wished they would get together and "talk it out".
A Vietnamese participant told her that she did not understand.
By avoiding contact, the families were avoiding the opportunity
for conflict. This was a traditional solution, and would
be equally characteristic of the Lao. An example of the
lengths to which leaders of opposing factions will go to
avoid open conflict is seen in the refusal of Khan (leader
of one faction) to visit his friend Kha because Booh (an
opposing faction's leader) lived in the apartment above

Kha. It was too chancey to visit because Khan might meet
Booh in the hallways or outside. This concern was never
directly voiced, of course.

All these factors can be illustrated in the matter
of Lao refugee leadership. Traditional Lao leadership
has been characterized as entourage, or a series of patron
and client relationships (Hanks, 1966). This structure
is characterized by individual connections maintained by
personal contact. Contact may be obtained by telephone,
visiting or letters. Patrons give time, money, goods and
energy to clients. Clients give friendship, loyalty, service
and hospitality in return. Clients are not bound to patrons
in any way and are free to end the relationship if they
perceive that another patron may offer more. This idea
of helping each other is also central to the Lao community
and is often repeated by the members of the community.
Many of the families who migrated to Columbus from other
areas came because they heard that the Lao here "really
helped each other". Because of the individualistic and
transient nature of these groupings, factionalism appears
to be a chronic problem of Lao leadership. This is perhaps
increased by the fact that, while in Laos patrons could
usually deliver promised rewards, here in the United States
Lao patrons frequently have limited access to resources
and cannot maintain followers as easily. This leads to
less encouragement for loyalty and more possibility for

factionalism. Leaders here are primarily educated, multilingual males who had connections with the United States during the war. Many come from families who were traditionally sources of leadership and were leaders in the refugee camps as well. It is interesting to note that three of the main leaders (and certainly the most powerful ones) in Columbus are actually Thai men married to Lao women. Women are not totally excluded from leadership. Visa was somewhat a patron in her own right although she continually arranged to defer credit to her husband for most of her accomplishments. By the end of the study, she had definitely been placed in a more subordinate role by the male leaders.[8]

This factionalism also has implications for the establishment of Mutual Assistant Associations for the Lao. Instead of truly representing the community, as Americans interpret the associations or the individuals running them, these associations tend to be the offspring of one particular faction. This is illustrated by the fact that, due to the ascendence at various times of various different factions, the local Lao group has had as many as three associations at the same time. Condominas (1975) mentions the use of a ceremonial hockey game as a symbolic political confrontation. It is suggestive that many of the Lao men in Columbus play soccer and were very interested in including a soccer match as part of the 1983 New Year Celebration -- an idea vetoed by the Cambodian Association.

On the other hand, there is, perhaps, a tendency to overrate this factionalism. It does exist and can reach violent proportions, but its basic reality is strongest solely within the leadership of the community. Only the leaders choose not to attend or to attend a formal party based on which group is sponsoring it -- the community itself gladly attends all parties and celebrations. It is also, ultimately, a male preoccupation. Women married to leaders of opposing factions are free to socialize and the wife of an opposing leader may even provide goods or services for the party given by another faction. This actually occurred during preparations for the 1983 Lao New Year celebration. The wife of one faction leader helped prepare food for the party sponsored by a rival leader's group. The daughter of one leader danced at the party although her father did not attend since it was sponsored by a rival group. In terms of day to day life, political factionalism is relatively unimportant for non-leaders. Respondents repeatedly named patrons from opposing factions when telling the researcher whom they sought out for help for different purposes.

The *Phi*, Buddha, and Christianity

Religious beliefs are very important to the Lao. Traditionally most Lao are Buddhist, although some converted to Christianity in Laos or came from Christian families.

The temple, or wat, serves as a focus for village life. Most Lao men spend some time in the temple as novices before marriage in order to bring honor to their family. In rural Laos there is a much greater emphasis placed on the idea of making merit (bun) than on avoidance of error (bap). Temple ceremonies serve as great sources of enjoyment for the people. The Buddhism is tempered with attention to the phi, or ancestral spirits. While it is unfair to characterize the phi as evil spirits, they are certainly not seen as benevolent. Certain circumstances of death, such as death during childbirth, are seen as causing particularly powerful and angry spirits.

Many ceremonies conducted by the monks at the temples actually are designed to appease the phi by providing offerings of food. For some groups, worship of the phi invoves personal and household spirits and household shrines (Potter, 1977). In rural Laos, while village spirits are considered more important, few keep shrines for personal or household spirits. The chaocham is in charge of ceremonies specifically directed toward the phi. The BaSi (also refered to as the soukhuan or soul tying) ceremony is one where people ask the phi for health and protection. Ingersoll (1966), in discussing fatalism in village Thailand, states that he suspects that the villagers may make specific supplications to the spirits. He also thinks that fatalism is somewhat overemphasized. Instead, he observed that villagers do indeed attempt to avoid misfortune and, only if they cannot do so, do they blame "fate".

Most of the above description remains valid for the Columbus Lao as well. There is not a local *wat* in Columbus, but the Columbus community is fortunate enough to have several men trained as Buddhist monks, a *momon*, and a *phi tai*. A *momon* is a man who can hear the *phi*. He is also a curer and can exorcise the *phi* if they take over a person. Visa compares the momon to a psychiatrist. A local woman was recently admitted to the mental health center. She was *phi bat* (insane, ruled by the *phi*). She manifested her illness by overdressing, using too much makeup, talking loudly and incessantly and laughing for no reason. She played with candles and broke dishes. She is doing better now as a result of injections from the center and the counseling of a *momon*. This instance shows a typical Lao pattern of incorporating new tecniques along with traditional methods of curing. Some of the Lao have adopted the coin rubbing of the Vietnamese. This practice which involves rubbing coins briskly across facial skin or the back or chest leaves abrasions on the skin and has been misinterpreted by some American health workers as evidence of abuse. The rubbing is thought to cure colds, headaches and other pains. One mother applied Vicks cold rub to her daughter's head when it was bumped. If a medicine works, its strength will be applied to many illnesses or injuries. There is great

faith in medications. Only women are *phi tai*. They, by
singing and dancing, can call the phi to find out what
the *phi* desire to have done and to shed light on the future.
The *phi tai* inherit this ability from close relatives.
Because of the availability of personnel the *BaSi* ceremony
is fairly accessible as is religious leadership. Most
homes have a Buddha picture on the living room wall or
a statue displayed on a shelf in the living room. Few
women make the flower and incense offerings they would
make if they lived in Laos. A frequent response to questions
of religion is that the people are still Buddhist but they
cannot follow Buddhism because there is no temple. Nonetheless
the idea of merit making continues. It is not important
to go to a temple — that would be nice and would make people
feel better. It is important how one lives his or her
life. One should be polite, gracious, and try to live
up to one's position as well as possible. The idea of
bettering one's present position is not really part of
the doctrine. Belief in the *phi* also continues although
the Lao do not discuss this openly with Americans. They
have found that Americans show some recognition and tolerance
of Buddhism, but have little respect for "spirits". In
addition, there is a feeling by some Lao that discussing
the *phi* with Americans might anger the *phi* or decrease
the potency of the *phi's* work. People continue to go to
the woods (thought to be a dwelling spot favored by the

*phi*) to talk to the *phi* and make personal supplications and offerings. The local Lao do feel special affection for the American holiday of Halloween. There is a similar holiday held in early autumn in Laos. In line with their understanding of the American holiday's meaning, the Lao call it "*nagka phi*" (mask of the *phi*).

The *BaSi* continues to be an important ceremony for marking recovery from illness, childbirth, leaving on a journey or any other important event in a person's life. Each *BaSi* will differ depending on the affluence of the host and the purpose of the ceremony. A description of one *BaSi*, held in conjunction with a Lao "American New Year" party follows. Everyone present, except the researcher, was Lao.[9]

The purpose of the *BaSi* was threefold: to celebrate the American New Year; to give thanks for the return of a woman from the hospital after surgery; and to celebrate her son's birthday. Birthdays are not traditionally celebrated in Laos, but the community in Columbus has instituted them for children and women. A large structure, also refered to as *BaSi*, three and a half feet in diameter and 4 feet tall, with conical protrusions had been constructed out of cardboard and covered with foil. It was placed in the center of the room. Flowers were placed in the tips of the cones. Pieces of yarn around 10 inches long were draped over the ends and bases of the cones. A large piece of yarn was strung around the entire structure. The structure sat in a basket full of sticky rice and eggs boiled in soy sauce. The second level had bananas and apples around the platform. The third had oranges and crackers. A plate with a whole boiled chicken was placed in front of the structure. When it was time to begin the *BaSi*, the structure was placed in the center of the living room floor mat. The birthday presents for the son were placed around the bottom of the structure. The woman and her husband kneeled in front of the structure. The woman wore an embroidered sash over one shoulder, pinned at the waist on the other side. Her husband and the *momon* each draped a towel over their left shoulder and pinned it at the waist. It looked very reminiscent of traditional robes that might be worn at the *wat*. The *momon* read a handwritten blessing asking the *phi* for health and protection. While he was chanting, conversation in the room continued, but at appropriate points the conversation would break and the entire group would bow their heads with hands clasped in front of their faces and respond. This blessing lasted about fifteen minutes. When the *momon* finished, everyone extended their hands toward the bottom of the lowest basket, palm up, and the *momon* dedicated the food to the spirits. The woman then held the plate of chicken while the *momon* repeated the dedication for this. Others nearby placed their hands, palm up, under her arms in a symbolic gesture of support

and community. The *momon* gave the plate to her husband
who repeated the process. At the same time an older woman
(a *phi tai*) did the same thing to a dish of apples and
oranges. The son was called to the mat and the birthday
cake placed in front of him. The other children were called
in and everyone sang "Happy Birthday". The children, cake
and presents then disappeared into the next apartment.
Everyone began taking pieces of yarn. A person would go
to an individual and take his/her hand, palm up. Others
would immediately place their hands under the receiver's
arm. The giver placed something (oranges, bananas, a drink,
etc.) in the receiver's palm and passed the yarn twice
under the hand, twice over the hand, and then tied the
yarn around the wrist. The yarn was tied underneath the
wrist and the ends of the yarn were "sealed" by rubbing
them together so that the spirits would not undo the good
wishes (yarn) of the giver. As one ties the string, he/she
must offer wishes for good luck, health, happiness, or
other favorable conditions. The receiver waits with the
other hand up by the side of the face, palm inward. The
wishes are acknowledged with a bow, clasped hands, and
a thank you. This continues until there are no more pieces
of yarn. Babies, children and the focal individual (i.e. the
woman recovering from surgery in this case) are popular
receivers. Children are often given money, which is tied
into the yarn at the wrist. Everyone present had an abundance

of yarn, and no one was overlooked. The strings are to be worn for three days after the ceremony. The BaSi is basically maintained in traditional form although its functions have expanded (e.g. used for birthdays now too).

American Christianity has had an effect on the Lao, however. Almost all Lao families interviewed were sponsored by a mainstream American church. As an extension of the patron-client relationship, the Lao feel compelled to attend the sponsor's church services and frequently to be baptized. Attendance usually decreases as interaction with the sponsor and aid from the sponsoring church decreases. Most Lao lump all Christian churches together. Most Lao could not remember the name, or denomination, of the church which originally sponsored them. Instead they might remember the name of the specific individuals with whom they had contact. One young man, Tha, who was being encouraged to become a lay minister by a Baptist church suggested that the church contact an older man who was presently a lay minister for a Methodist church. Tha's concern was that his age, educational experience and family background, made him unacceptable as a leader according to traditional Lao criteria. He saw no conflict in the fact that his suggested replacement was affiliated with a different Christian denomination. Repeatedly, the researcher heard that it did not make any difference where one went to talk to God -- church, wat, it was all the same. Visa also drew a parallel between the *phi* and the Holy Spirit: "it is all the same thing, we just call it differently. There is God and there are spirits." For this reason many Lao feel tolerant (although not comfortable) attending church and see attendance as part of establishing valuable patron-client relationships with Americans. Once rewards from these relationships end, so does church attendance. Some Lao, however, believe strongly that going into a church would end their spiritual protection. One Mutual Assistance Association was hurt by its association with a local Protestant church. People felt uncomfortable having to accept the religion (as a duty owed to the patron who was a Lao lay minister) along with the organization.

The Lao are also not very comfortable with groups given to heavy prosetylization. One local church sends a couple to visit Lao families in the Metropolitan Housing area every Tuesday evening. They sit and try to talk with the Lao then leave after urging attendance at church functions. Conversation is difficult, to say the least, since the couple speak little Lao, and the Lao adults speak little English. During the course of one visit the couple said three times: "We love our Lao families". To this the Lao simply smile and nod politely. The people will accept help in finding jobs, but little else. As is customary, they smile, nod and promise to attend a picnic or service, then simply do not show up for it.

The refugees have maintained traditional religious attitudes in terms of Buddhism, merit making and the *phi*. Even the Lao refugees who practiced a form of Christianity in Laos participate in *BaSi* and other traditional ceremonies. American Christian churches are seen in more instrumental than religious terms -- that is, as potential sources for American patrons.

## Children

Children have always been desired by Lao. As mentioned before, everyone loves a baby. Children of both sexes are desired. Men tend to emphasize the desire for male offspring. Lao society accords males a higher status than females and accordingly a son is highly valued. This was clearly illustrated when Khan was recounting an episode designed to show the ineptitude of Thong, a leader of an opposing faction. Thong, he claimed, had not known what to do and had taken too long getting a woman who was in labor to the hospital. By the time she got to the hospital the baby had died -- "and it was a boy too". In spite of this seeming preference for males, Lao women (and men) are interested in female offspring as well. Children of both sexes must help around the house and, although females are required to continue this until they marry, this extra household workforce is not the reason for the desire for females. Due to the uxori-parentilocal residence patterns characteristic of the Lao, it is a daughter (usually the youngest) and her husband who ultimately inherit a family's farm and, in return, care for parents in their old age. This quest for a daughter is important. One woman told the researcher that she had seven sons. She became pregnant again and went to the temple and asked for a daughter. She was successful. Visa, who has two sons, says she would become pregnant again immediately if it would be a daughter. If it were a boy, "I would push it back inside and say I don't want it." Another woman with three boys agreed saying "If it were a boy, I would not look at it. Boys are so terrible." In order to tell whether one will have a boy or a girl, the pregnant woman stands a baby on her stomach. If the baby (boy or girl) stands on both feet, the unborn baby is a boy. Standing on one foot indicates a girl. This is because men are stronger than women, according to Visa. It is interesting that while Lao have different expectations for males and females, many Lao names may be either masculine or feminine. No offense is taken if a small boy is mistaken for a girl or vice versa.

If a woman has twins, the first one delivered is considered the younger and the second delivered is the older because it must have been in the womb longer. Twins are given names that are similar in sound (e.g. Pan and Pon) and are considered special people. They may become important, lucky and/or rich and are destined to help others. Other birth indicators of this same special status are a birth where the umbilical cord is around the baby's neck or where the cord slides across the one shoulder and under the other arm (similar to the position of the sashes worn by monks or by women in traditional costume).

Children are usually taken to a fortune teller when they are young so that parents may know how best to facilitate their futures. Visa, for example, recalls that she was told that she would marry a man who corresponds to her husband's personality and physical description. She was also told she would go far from her home, but be successful and help others.

While breastfeeding is the traditional source of nourishment for Lao babies, bottle feeding is rapidly replacing it in the United States. This is especially true for primaparous mothers or those with limited mothering experience while in Laos. The Lao believe that all Americans bottle feed and indeed one woman stopped breastfeeding her nine month old son because her American sponsor told her Americans did not do that. She switched her son to a bottle which he still takes at 26 months of age -- a practice that many Americans would still disapprove. A more commonly cited reason for bottlefeedings was the mother's need to return to work. The fact that breastfeeding is still regarded as preferable, at least among adults in their mid-twenties and older, did surface repeatedly in response to the researcher's breast feeding her own son. She was told frequently by older Lao (men and women) that she did "it like we do it. This makes healthy babies with strong bodies and good minds. You will see". Breastfeeding in Laos traditionally continued for several years and a woman might still be nursing one child when another was born. The preferred mode of nourishment (bottle versus breast) may be under conversion, but attitudes toward when to feed and how long to feed do not seem to be. Whether using the bottle or breast, a Lao mother feeds whenever the child evidences interest in food or dissatisfaction. Any evidence of fussing by a child is likely to be greeted with an offering of food. During one visit a two and one half year old child seemed upset when his ten month old sister received a bottle. His mother promptly filled another bottle with Orange Crush and gave it to him. Frequently even three year olds were observed sharing baby food with a younger sibling or taking a bottle -- usually filled with a soft drink. It was not uncommon to see three year olds using pacifiers. All children (as do Lao adults) eat and sleep where and when they feel like it. For the breastfeeding mother there are no restrictions or uneasiness regarding what is seen as a natural function of motherhood. The Lao do not regard the breast as primarily sexual in nature, but rather as a source of nourishment for the baby. Anytime or anywhere the baby wants to nurse is the right time and place. This also extends to older children. They are free to request food or (as is more usual) prepare their own food whenever they wish and no one is "put to bed". When children are tired, they sleep. Older children are more likely to feel tired and go to the bedroom before sleeping; younger children basically fall asleep where they are and are carried to bed by adults.

Excretory functions and toilet training are treated in a similarly relaxed manner. Young children frequently wear only shirts and any indiscretions are simply cleaned up without comment. Underpants may be used on even very young children, more as a concession to American sensitivities than for any other function. These are simply changed if the child urinates or defecates. Mothers who have had babies in the United States are acquainted with diapers and use them on infants. No emphasis is put on toilet training by parents and the children basically train themselves -- most by the age of three or three and one half years of age. Parents explain that the children eventually get tired of wet pants and decide to stay clean. The Lao are aware that Americans do not approve of diaperless/pantless children and, while children are free to roam the home this way, they are retrieved and "appropriately" attired if they venture outside or if Americans are visiting.

The youngest child usually stays close to the mother or father until around three years of age. At this time they switch to a greater association with peers. If another sibling arrives before this time, they will gravitate to the peer group at an earlier age. This emphasis and dependence on other children is fostered from the beginning of life. Babies are shown to each other. They are placed close together on a mat and held so that their eyes are directed toward each other while adults formally introduce them. Touching of one another and watching each other is encouraged and greeted with pleasure by the adults. The researcher was told over and over that she had a "good" baby because he did not fuss and anyone could hold him. Lao babies are held and played with by everyone. No Lao would ask if she/he could hold a Lao baby -- the baby is simply taken and played with, usually by the women or older children. No Lao mother, should such an unexpected request be made, would think of denying someone the pleasure of holding the child. Other children, especially girls, are supposed to entertain the babies so that adults may work and talk. Should the baby become upset, she/he is returned to the mother or father.

Older children function within a group of peers. They are responsible for themselves and are largely ignored by the adults. The oldest children, male or female, are expected to care for the younger. A good example of this was seen during the first contact the researcher had with the Lao community. A group of children were playing outside when one of them cut his hand. The older children immediately

went inside and got first aid supplies. The one girl's
father asked what had happened, was told, and went back
to his conversation with visitors. The boy's hand was
bandaged by the children. At no point did any adult look
at the cut, nor deal with the situation. The Lao commented
frequently that they liked the way the Americans watched
the Lao children in school -- even on the playground.
One woman said "we do not watch them like that, you know,
but it is nice that the school does." The idea of caring
for younger children begins with the birth of the subsequent
sibling. Mistreatment of the baby is gently stopped.
Anger is discouraged. The older children are incorporated
into the daily care of the baby and, of course, the one
who used to be the youngest seeks solace from older siblings
upon being deposed. It was not at all unusual to see four
year olds holding or carrying a two and one half year old
sibling who was hurt or upset. Young children, focused
on their mothers, tend to groom the mother a lot, stroking
the hair and playing with it. Older girls groom each other,
fixing hair and makeup.

Phillips (1965) mentions children being given to other
families in Thai society and feels that this practice causes
psychological problems for the children involved. Borrowing
of children is also common among the Lao in Columbus.
Most Columbus borrowing is of a very temporary nature,
consisting of children staying with different families

overnight or for a few days. One family did, however, lend its ten year old son to a Thai friend. The Thai woman, married to an American, was childless (this may have been by choice). She took a liking to the son and told the family she was lonely. After a period of six or seven months the community pressured her to give the child back - only.because she was not sending him to school and American authorities were threatening the parents with legal action.

Some parents left a child in Laos with a grandmother because it was the grandmother who was closest to the child. One woman told me that her oldest son cried and screamed when told the family was leaving Laos. She could not hurt him like that so she allowed him to stay with his grandmother, although it made her very sad. Another man mentioned that he had given his second daughter to his brother and brother's wife because they had no children. One woman brought her grandson to Columbus with her, while his parents remained in Laos. These examples are aspects of the same traditional pattern noted by Phillips. In Columbus, children are also free to come and go as they please and frequently stay at other people's houses. There is no evidence that there are any psychological problems associated with this local pattern. It seems that it is simply a logical extension of the importance of the extended family, the need for children to care for one in one's old age, and the importance of the peer group. A child may easily develop a particularly close relationship with a grandmother and, since the Lao do not feel it is right to force anyone -- even a child -- the child may choose to stay with that person instead of the nuclear family. Likewise a couple with no children would make any child that lived with them feel very wanted. One does not feel unwanted by parents, but instead one desires prolonged contact with another adult or the all important peers.

The peers are very important to the child and, as every society makes divisions on the basis of factors such as age and sex, it seems legitimate to characterize the Lao as having an adult world and a children's world -- each with their own set of rules and behaviors. While a politeness and respect are expected in the presence of adults, within the peer group things are very relaxed. Play tends to be active and noisy and much like that of the youngsters' American counterparts. The major apparent difference is the role of the older children as caretakers for the younger children.

Discipline traditionally is verbal and more by example then by direction (LeBar and Suddard, 1967). Phillips (1965) sees discipline in the Thai village he studied as nonexistent. He states that parents ritually correct children, then drop the matter and children may do what they wish. This has not been observed by the researcher. Although to American eyes discipline may be hard to discern, it

is present. As previously stated the Lao feel that even
children should be respected and prefer to give them encouragement and examples of good behavior, rather than to directly
instruct or force compliance. In the group studied, disciplinary attitudes fell into one of two categories. Most of
the older Lao, or those who had learned parenting in Lao
traditional society used primarily verbal methods of discipline. Specifically, they would talk to their children
or try to distract very young children into a more acceptable
pastime. If they became very upset with the children,
they might speak loudly to them, an action they felt was
rude and wrong. Many of the younger parents who had not
experienced the more troublesome years of toddlerhood parenting
in the traditional society used more physical means such
as spanking (*ti*). This is still usually a light spank
and either on the offending part of the anatomy (e.g. a
hand that is breaking something) or on the child's bottom.
One Lao woman who spanked her children reacted with shock
when she saw an American woman shake her child and hit
him hard on the back. Some more traditionally oriented
parents have occasionally spanked their children, but regard
it with a great deal of ambivalence and guilt. For example,
one woman told the researcher that she spanked her child
once, but "it made my hand hurt". Other women made similiar
statements. The more accultured Lao feel under some pressure
to make their children conform to American expectations

which include overt and definite punishment (in the Lao perception). The researcher does not wish to paint an overly optimistic picture in terms of discipline. Domestic violence toward women and children does exist in both traditional Lao society and the local Lao community, but it has seemed minimal among the group studied. Only one case of wife abuse (of which the researcher was aware) occurred during the study. It was attributed to the husband's drinking problem. Although stress has undoubtedly increased for the refugees, cultural alternatives to violence do exist. Specifically an abused wife (or child) may simply utilize her social network and mobility to leave. This follows traditional patterns of conflict avoidance. It also minimizes the likelihood of intervention by American authorities which may have unpleasant ramifications. The one case that occurred resulted in a court case to determine whether or not to remove the couple's children into state custody. The couple was able to retain custody and subsequently moved from the area.

Children are expected to help around the house and with younger siblings as soon as they are able to do so. Most infractions revolve around these duties. Common complaints from parents include: the children do not do what they are told; they do not stay around the house the way they should; they do not help with their jobs; they fight with each other.

When children are upset, the parents will frequently sympathize with the child for the child's anger. Many times the researcher observed a parent holding a crying child or stroking his/her back saying "sorry, sorry, sorry" (in English).

All the parents wanted their children to learn English and to learn about America and Americans; but almost all also wanted their children to remember that they were Lao. They wanted the children to speak Lao (and a few of the better educated ones also wanted the children to read and write Lao) and to "be Lao". To be Lao was described as being polite, respectful, to care for aged parents and to embody other Lao traditional qualities. Many expressed a desire for their children to visit Laos at some future time so they might see their country, the parents' old home, and the relatives left behind. A frequent joking response that was made when this was said was "you tell them where you hid the money jar". This is in reference to the practice of burying family treasures somewhere on one's farm so that it is safe from other people. Due to the hurried and dangerous circumstances of most of the local refugees' flights from home, any treasures were left where they were.

The Thirst for Knowledge

Education has always been a factor influencing status in Lao society. This does not, however, mean that everyone desires an extensive education. As mentioned previously, the idea of *bun* involves doing the best at one's particular station in life. A farmer does not need to go to a university. The educational system in Laos was set up by the French and entailed a primary school system followed by *"college"* (secondary school), temple training, or other vocational training. The primary methods of instruction were lecture and rote memorization. A person did not progress almost automatically from grade to grade as in the American system and would not begin school until the age of seven or eight[10]. The folk test designed to verify that a child was ready to enroll in school was to have the child raise his arm above the head, then lower it over the top of the head and try to touch his/her ear on the other side. Success at this task meant readiness for school.

Most adults in the study had little interest in adult education. They did not attend English classes regularly or any other kind of training program. A few did enroll in CETA training programs or technical institutes in an attempt to gain skills, but these few already had had more extensive education in Laos; were from urban areas; had some facility in the English language; and were members of the local leaders' families or close associates. In general, adults took vocational training only if there was a specific job available (e.g. women learned to operate sewing machines because several local companies were actively hiring Lao women as stitchers). For most, the philosophy was that they simply wanted enough money to survive: to get a television, a car and enough food. At this point, the individuals would "plateau out" (Van Esterik, 1983:8).

Education for children was another matter. The Lao clearly recognize that education and the acquisition of skills is central to the question of their children's future. Education is seen as the children's primary duty. This attitude has the potential for causing problems for educators since they may interpret the parents' lack of participation in the children's education as lack of interest. In reality, it is due to the parents' perception of education as between the child and the school, and of themselves as unskilled and so unable to help. The Lao would never openly question the wisdom of an educator or a school policy, although they might have some private doubts. When questioned directly most denied any concerns over subject matter, but several of the older Lao, in casual conversation with the researcher, did voice concern over the anatomy lessons given to children, especially daughters, in the schools. "This is for doctors, not for girls," was a common refrain. In a similar fashion, when their child is held back or has problems, parents feel it is because the child does not study hard enough.

In typical Lao fashion, parents will agree to a parent-teacher conference, and then not show up because they feel that they have nothing to say and they would not understand because of the language barrier anyway. Some of the Lao families who were in other areas of the United States previously mentioned the use of weekend or after-school classes for the refugee children where information could be re-explained in the child's own language and help given with homework. Several of the men in the local community had taught in the temple or schools in Laos and were interested in finding jobs with the Columbus public schools as teachers' aides. Most parents felt that, while older children had a language problem, most younger children caught on quickly and had no real language problems. One woman told the researcher proudly that her daughter's teacher had said that her daughter did better than a lot of American children in school. The woman attributed this to the fact that her daughter studied so hard.

The children have problems because their politeness (smiling and nodding agreement) is frequently interpreted by American teachers as understanding when there is none. Their cultural background ill-equips them to deal with learning situations where children are supposed to discuss and debate issues with teachers. Learning is listening rather than participating. Typical American nonverbal behavior such as patting a child on the head may be very upsetting. Many of the younger children seemed to particularly like mathematics -- the researcher wonders if this is due to minimization of language problems and the fact that mathematics is frequently taught in a fashion more similar to Lao tradition (i.e. the teacher instructs the students who listen) and the use of rote memorization.

Older children, particularly males, seem to drop out due to language difficulties and the desire for employment rather frequently. Younger children show a greater variety in success rate. All the parents interviewed would prefer for their children to get A's or B's, but realistically would accept C's. Most seemed forgiving of those older children who had limited success. Younger children who were held back were frequently considered lax in studying. One aspect of the American school system does perplex the Lao. As one man, talking to the researcher, put it

> In Laos you stay in a grade until you learn what
> you need to know. Here, you put children in
> grades by age, not by what they know. This is
> hard, especially for our children who have never
> been to school and do not speak English. They
> are expected to learn much at once.

Van Esterik (1983) suggests that Lao parents are easily impressed and in some ways the researcher concurs. The parents were very proud of any award or piece of paper brought home from school by the child. On the other hand, parents in the study tended to feel the children did not study enough and were concerned about grades. Education for children was considered of primary importance. Perhaps the fact that they do not share the goals of many middle-class Americans may have influenced Van Esterik's observations. Most do not expect their children to go to college -- they will be happy if they graduate from high school and see vocational training as an acceptable alternative to even this. Being practical, the Lao realize they have neither the time nor the money to put a child through college -- they will need the child to obtain a job and contribute income to the family as soon as possible. But over and over again the researcher was told "education is the future, without education our children will not get jobs. Without a job, they cannot live".

Being Merry

For the local Lao the easiest, most inexpensive way of having fun is also very traditional -- go fishing or have a picnic. These activities are usually spontaneous although they may be planned. The children love to swim and those who spent any amount of time in Laos beyond a few months of age probably learned to swim before they walked. Men are incessant smokers. Younger women do not smoke, but old women may. They usually prefer to unroll the tobacco from a cigarette and chew it instead. Food preparation, when done by a group of women, takes on the air of a party, with gossiping, tasting and joking seasoning the work. Every home is decorated with Thai film posters, calendars (of Chinese or other Asian origin), family pictures, pictures of Lao royalty, and/or certificates from children's schools. A few have posters showing the Lao alphabet. A local Thai merchant rented a theatre one weekend each month to show Thai films -- this started in December of 1982. The Lao go to these films as do the Thai because many understand Thai and the Thai culture and values are similar to Lao culture. This is a more expensive form of entertainment so not everyone goes every month. Almost every home has a television and a stereo (only two families in the study did not have a television). Most with children over the age of four have a video game set. The television is almost always turned on. Men like to watch boxing in particular, and other sports in general (football is not considered very exciting however). During the day the set is just left on whatever channel anyone has watched. The older children (and the women) like MTV, a music video channel, and Solid Gold, a pop music dance show. Younger children love the cartoons, superhero shows, kung fu shows, Dukes of Hazzard, A-Team and like genre. Along this same line, camouflage army clothes are very popular with the Lao males (particularly adolescents) as is motorcycle para-phernalia. A motorcycle was a common mode of transportation for many of these people in Laos and remains popular for young men in Columbus. Girls, in keeping with the Lao ideas of modesty which emphasize the lower body, rarely wear shorts. Most of the Lao women wear traditional clothing at home and long pants or skirts or dresses when they go to work. Female children may also wear traditional clothing at home, or pants, skirts or dresses. Traditional female informal attire consists of a long wrap around skirt of cotton and any shirt or pullover desired. Bras are not frequently worn. For more formal occasions (like New Year's Festival) traditional wrap around skirts of cotton and silk with hand embroidery are worn along with a cotton and silk embroidered sash which goes over the left shoulder and around the chest.

Adult males dress in American style and frequently wear shorts in hot weather. Footwear for everyone is light, consisting mainly of thongs or sandals, and is usually removed upon entering a house or apartment. This is true even in cold weather. Women and older girls like open toed, high heel sandals for formal wear.

Parties are a favorite form of entertainment for the local Lao community. Informal parties grow out of normal visiting with the addition of music and sufficient guests. Formal parties, on the other hand, are elaborate affairs for which tickets are sold and require a vast amount of preparation. Informal parties include birthday parties for children and for women, and most other gatherings. Most local Lao celebrate three American holidays. Many put up Christmas trees and lights for Christmas (but do not give presents, and may leave the plastic tree and lights up all year); children go out for Halloween while parents give out candy; and a few Lao have turkey (albeit usually boiled rather than roasted) for Thanksgiving. The birthday parties for the Lao women were actually instigated by Visa (long before this research began) as a means of helping the Lao to learn American customs. This process was stopped during the research as unemployment increased and many families were financially unable to provide the expected hospitality at the party. Informal birthday parties for children and women did continue according to each family's personal means and desires. A description of a formally organized birthday party, an American New Year's party, and a formal Lao New Year's Celebration follow.

Chanh's Birthday Party: December 12, 1982, 7:00pm.
As the men enter, they shake hands with the other men; women nod to each other and speak a greeting. Everyone takes off their shoes as they enter. Shoes are removed as a sign of respect. It would be insulting to bring dirt into someone's home. It is also practical. If one eats on floor mats, one would prefer not to have dirty shoes on them first. The men all sit on one side of the living room -- most on a large mat on the floor, some on chairs. They are watching boxing on television and drinking beer. As each man comes into the room he is offered a small glass of whiskey which is passed to him and then to each man

already in the room. There is almost a competitive aspect to the drinking. The women sit on the other side of the room. Most are drinking Pepsi although some eventually drink beer. After an hour or so, one of the local leaders (Mr. Thong) starts on the presents which have been stacked on a table in the corner of the room. Chanh stands by the table full of gifts and hands them, one by one, to Mr. Thong. Visa also stands by the table. Visa tells who the present is from and reads the card if it is appropriate. Many are not, but may be for any occasion -- the picture being more important than the message. Mr. Thong then opens the present and displays each one, keeping up a running commentary on the presents and the givers. Most presents are towels, drinking glasses and blankets -- all very practical and useful. The Lao take many baths -- actually showers. Although they use the word bath, the Lao do not approve of sitting in standing water and consider this unclean. It is also unclean to wash the head with water in which one has sat. Drinking glasses are needed in endless number so that one always has enough to offer visitors refreshment. Blankets are expensive and in short supply among a people used to tropical climates. The commentary offered may be in praise of the item or may be of more ribald nature. For example, when one blanket was opened, Mr. Thong said (in Lao) "What is this for? It covers your whole body. Maybe they will make love under it". He laughed and the audience joined in. The commentary and gift are greeted with applause, laughter and, occasionally catcalls. After all the presents are opened people stay and visit late into the night. A bowl of soup containing rice noodles, bean sprouts, mint, pork parts, coconut juices, pepper and spices was given to each person. In addition, the men were given a plate with thin slices of pork, a plate of lettuce and bean sprouts, and a bowl of hot sauce for all to share. There may or may not be birthday cake (usually supplied by "Kroger's"11) for an adult's party, but there will always be one for a child. In any case, the cake is only eaten by the children -- who devour it in a matter of seconds.

A Lao "American New Year" party: January 1, 1983, 1:00p.m. The living room was decorated with streamers and balloons. The women were on a mat outside of the kitchen (in what Americans would consider the dining alcove) preparing baskets of sticky rice, rice noodles, chicken, vegetables and spices. After everyone expected had arrived, the group all went into the living room and sat on the floor mat and a BaSi ceremony was held. After the BaSi, visiting resumed. The men were drinking beer and wine and whiskey. They offered these to the women as well. A few women accepted beer, but most refused it and all refused the wine and whiskey. The men would insist and eventually the women would accept it. The drink was either taken with much

giggling or, just as frequently, spilled on the floor --
deliberately, the researcher suspects. Everytime the men
offered the women a drink, they would say "Happy New Year".
One of the men told the researcher, "This is your custom,
not ours!" Nonetheless, they seemed to enjoy it. The
children all ran out in the hall or over to another apartment
after the BaSi. The food was brought out next. Sticky
rice was scooped out of the baskets, rolled in a ball,
dipped in a sauce and eaten. The sauce on this occasion
was a mixture of chicken, soy sauce, hot peppers and garlic.
There were also plates with pieces of boiled chicken, and
lettuce and chives -- all eaten communally with the fingers.
There were two large bowls of soup made with chicken parts
and vegetables. Each bowl contained two spoons and these
were also used communally. As soon as the food was finished,
everything was cleared away into the kitchen and the mat
was taken up. Lao music was played on a tape deck and
women and men began to dance. The dance was a traditional
circle dance involving a measured, walking gait, slow turns,
and hand gestures. The drinking by the men continued as
did the offering of drinks to the women and things got
noisier. The men pulled the women out on the floor to
dance. As drinking continued the body movements in the
dance got freer and clowning around began. A woman would
hit a man with an exaggerated hip movement (or might not

even make any actual contact, just making the gesture alone), and the man staggered away as if hit squarely.

In accordance with the Lao interpretation of American New Year customs a man went to each person saying "Happy New Year" and offered each, in turn a drink from the same glass of beer. The beer was to be consumed in one gulp. He would not take no for an answer. For women the glass was filled around two inches (and many took more than one gulp to drink it). For men it was filled four to six inches. And the talking, drinking and dancing continued, well into the night.

Formal Lao New Year Party: May 7, 1983
This particular party was held in conjunction with the Cambodian Mutual Assistance Association. The Cambodian Mutual Assistance Association (CMAA) took the gate receipts and money from drinks and the Lao Mai Association provided food and took the money paid for that. The affair was held in a local college auditorium and cafeteria -- one that had been used by the CMAA previously. The show took place in the auditorium and then moved to the cafeteria for dinner and dancing. The formal program read as follows:

4:00 PM   Guests of Honor arrived

5:00      Introduction, Chairperson - President of the CMAA

5:02      Singing United States National Anthem & Laotian
          National Anthem

5:05      Opening Remarks, Executive Director of CMAA

| 5:07 | Presentation: President of the CMAA - Speech in English |
|---|---|
| 5:15 | Executive Director of the CMAA -- Speech in Cambodian |
| 5:20 | Chairperson of the Lao Mai Association -- Speech in English |
| 5:25 | President of the Lao Mai Association -- Speech in Lao |
| 5:30 | BACI (BaSi) (Laotian Cultural Ceremony) |
| 5:50 | Cambodian Classical Dances |
| 6:05 | Laotian Classical Dances |
| 6:15 | Cambodian Classical Dance |
| 6:20 | Laotian Music by bamboo flute |
| 6:30 | Cambodian Folk Dances |
| 7:00 | Kung Fu Karate show |
| 7:10 | Cambodian Folk Dance |
| 7:15 | Laotian and H'mong Costume Show |
| 7:30 | DINNER |
| 8:30 | Laotian and Cambodian Circle Dances and music to live band |

Things basically went according to the program except that the speeches ran longer than their allotted times and everything started around one half hour later than expected. The karate and kung fu show never showed up either. The Lao had lobbied unsuccessfully for a soccer match to be included as an afternoon activity. The CMAA was basically in control and vetoed the idea. For the purposes of the festival the local Lao community organized a dance troupe of girls (thirteen girls from the ages of seven through sixteen, with most being in the younger years). The girls came from many different families and the daughters of several rival patrons were involved. The girls practiced five or six hours every week for three months before the festival. Traditional dances that the girls would have learned as part of their school education in Laos were taught by an older woman who knew many dances and the oldest girl, who was considered the troupe's actual teacher. Several of the young women who had received their education in Laos also helped out. Every practice session required lots of refreshments for the dancers during breaks. Traditional cotton and silk skirts and sashes were worn by the dancers. The feet were bare and the hair was worn coiled on top of the head. The dances all involved slow, deliberate, precision hand and foot movements and were fascinating to watch. Since the festival, the troupe has remained intact, expanded its repertoire of dances and performed for several other Lao and American functions. The community hopes to get support from the Ohio Council of the Arts so that the troupe may continue and even expand to include a boys troupe as well.

# CHAPTER FIVE

THE NEW ADDITION - FOCUS ON WOMEN

## Structural Status Versus Cultural Status of Women

One must decide what issues are relevant to determine the position of women. Van Esterik (1982) has organized a book around the question of women's status in Southeast Asian cultures. She points out that it has been accepted that women enjoy high status in this area, but that little research has been done to support (or contradict) the cliche'. Van Esterik (1982) has chosen to focus on religious, domestic and economic aspects of women's lives.

Theravada Buddhism is widespread in Southeast Asia and is the major religion in Laos. Buddhist doctrine defines women as "inherently lower in status than men, and women are barred by sex from aspiring to the roles to which the greatest virtue attaches" (Keyes, 1977:161). Men are, ideologically, superior to women. Women are associated with nurturance, and attachment; while men are associated with the valued detachment from worldly things and supramundane power. This leads to low status culturally.

Bourguignon (1980) focused on three approaches to the study of women in various cultures. These are:

119

1) sexual division of labor, subsistence strategies and women's status

2) the question of the utility of the concepts of domestic/private/public domains, and their definition

3) culture change as it effects the position of women

These categories match Van Esterik's (1982) approach well. Bourguignon (1980) also emphasizes religion in dealing with these categories of study and Van Esterik (1982), focuses on questions of domain, economics and culture change as well. Bourguignon (1980) points out that women's tasks are highly diverse cross-culturally and yet they share a common core revolving around household and management including production activities, rearing of children, and cooking. Laderman (1982) and Hull (1982) focus on the meaning of women's domestic activities. Although women may be culturally devalued by religous tradition, they are necessary for men to reach significant status positions, and women know this (Bourguignon, 1980). For example, a male Lao patron can only meet his obligations for hospitality through the expertise and energy of his wife.

In addition Laderman (1982) and Hull (1982) both deal with women as integrating families into wider community networks. Potter (1977) focuses on the significance of women and of affinal ties in ordering a Thai village. Boone (1980) mentions that Cubans in Washington substitute networks and grapevines which are largely female for tightly knit neighborhoods in order to maintain a sense of community. Lao women also serve a network-forming function in the local community which -- while not entirely dispersed -- is not completely geographically clustered.

Women in Southeast Asia have been involved in marketing and entrepreneurial endeavors traditionally -- perhaps a preadaption of roles (Bourguignon, 1980) that encourages success in the new host economy. Bourguignon (1980) offers a quote which, while referenced in particular to accounts of Eskimo life, may be expanded to any culture:

> locating the center and the margins of a society
> . . . appears to depend on the position of the
> observer                                    (p 339)

This brings one to a consideration of domains. The public domain has usually been considered male and the private considered domestic and female. There are extensive problems of definition with the various domains[1] and other domains have been proposed in addition. An interesting extension is that of ethnic public domain versus national public domain, (Boone in Bourguignon, 1980). It is proposed that there may be nonformalized roles for women in the ethnic domain that would be incomprehensible in the national domain. A nonformalized role is private in the sense that it is based on personal interaction but takes place in a public (non-domestic) setting. The Lao women who may be community leaders in matters which do not involve outsiders and which are not considered political may be an example of this.

Van Esterik (1982:12) points out that the question of what is public and what is private in Southeast Asian cultures may be problematical.

> Domestic acts such as food preparation and presenta-
> tion may be public perfomances . . . the domestic
> domain encompasses the social sphere, and women
> play an important role in social activities.

Such is certainly the case for the Lao, as will be seen.

The idea of the relative isolation of females and sociability of males must also be questioned -- for the Lao it is the women who are more communally organized and the men who are more individualistic and competitive. Men are also more concerned with the formalities and ceremony of a situation. In fact, they frequently get bogged down in these details and never actually accomplish their goal. Women are more task-oriented and will work toward a goal without worrying if the process is absolutely formally correct. These attitudes can be seen in Lao parties. Spontaneous parties may be started by either males or females, but are frequently an outgrowth of the normal hospitality provided by females. The New Year's celebration, on the other hand, was carefully planned step by step by the men. Each dignitary had to have his/her time to speak in the proper order; national anthems had to be sung; every detail of form and formality was scrutinized.

Lastly one must deal with change. Bourguignon (1980:339) points out that

work opportunities in the public sector for women
who previously did not have them does not necessarily
give them greater freedom or increase their power,
authority, or status

In fact it may decrease status or have little effect upon
it. Hoskins (1976) points out that wage earning for Vietnamese
women is a logical extension of traditional activities and,
since money is all put into a household fund, wage earning
does not in itself affect the position of women. It appears
much the same for the Lao in the local community. The addition
of wage labor for women has not altered their roles to any
great extent at this time.

A Composite Daily Round

The following daily round is a composite and applies
to unemployed Lao women in Columbus. The local Lao involved
in this study all live in apartments or duplexes. The living
room is the central room of the house and contains a couch
and perhaps a chair or two (given by sponsors or replacements
of ones given by sponsors). A large woven mat covers the
floor and there may also be a low table. The television
occupies a prominent space, as does the stereo. A small
kitchen table may be pushed against a wall in the dining
area, but usually there are no chairs around it. The table
was most likely a gift from an American sponsor and is rarely,
if ever, used for eating -- most eating is done sitting
on the mat on the floor. The kitchen will also have a woven
mat on the floor (if there is room) and this is where most

food preparation occurs. If there is no room in the kitchen, the area outside the kitchen will be used (hall or dining room). Bedrooms show more variability. A more acculturated individual with more means may have a bed and dresser in each bedroom. Children frequently share beds and in some families mats or mattresses replace beds. Some of the older, more traditionally oriented Lao try to place beds with the head of the bed in an east or north orientation as dictated by Buddhist doctrine; but space confines do not always allow this. Most families do not concern themselves with such things at all.

One gets up when the spirit moves. Children in school are responsible for getting up, dressing themselves, and finding breakfast (probably cereal from a box). Breakfast for oneself and husband consists of *kopia* (boiled rice) or maybe some food left over from dinner. The house must then be straightened. If there are pre-school age children at home they may help with the making of beds and other chores or play at home or with neighbors. Morning is an unhurried time for cleaning.

Lunch may be a communal affair and is better if it is. Anytime is a good time for visiting and, if the weather is nice, the neighborhood Lao women may sit outside and have a picnic. They will talk and prepare the food and eat it together. Hands are rarely idle. Everyone, even children can help to prepare the food -- children are particularly good at tasting the food while it is being prepared. The lunch will have the ever-present sticky rice (kau), and maybe soup of chicken broth and green onions with meat added. The meat may be pork, chicken or beef -- but for a women's meal it will probably be the more available and less expensive chicken or pork. A hot sauce of garlic and chili will be available. The sticky rice is taken in a ball with the fingers and dipped into the sauce. Eating utensils include large bowls, chopsticks and tablespoon-sized spoons. After lunch, everyone helps to clean up dishes.

Now there is more time for visiting, taking care of children who are returning from school, and perhaps a shopping trip or doing the laundry. Even while visiting, the Lao use their hands continually. Someone may sew, tend a baby, fix another's hair, or just handle a toy or other object. If it is a nice day, laundry will probably be washed in the sink and hung out to dry. If one is lucky enough to own a washer and dryer, or knows someone who does, one may use these machines. If the weather (and time) permits, air drying is preferred. All things go better with friends and tasks are rarely undertaken alone if a neighbor or friend can be found to participate. Fishing is a favorite pastime in the summer and there are some nearby creeks that are utilized for this purpose. The women and children may go fishing by themselves or with the men in a family group.

Dinner, again, may be a cooperative effort. Instead of the women preparing the meal together eating as they work, several women may come to one woman's house to help with the cooking. The men will sit in the living room (perhaps around a table, but more likely on a mat on the floor) and the women will serve them. The women will eat, talking and laughing, in the kitchen while preparing and serving the food. The women are free to sit with the men and eat, but prefer the more interesting conversation and company in the kitchen. Dinner will include some meat (chicken, pork, beef, frog, or fish); vegetables (either mixed with noodles in a soup or as a plate of fresh vegetables); sticky rice; and hot sauces. Dishes may be communal or individual.

After dinner the family may visit other families, or friends may drop by and adults will sit and talk -- men with men and women with women -- while children play in halls, other apartments, or outside. Unlike the visiting during the day when women come and go freely, in the evening women are more likely to remain at home unless the entire family (including the husband) is going to visit. The television will be on, as it has been whenever anyone is in the house. Unless there is a boxing match (men love it) or a show like Dallas (which some Lao women seem to find interesting), the adults will probably not be watching. Perhaps J.R. Ewing reminds the Lao of an unscrupulous, but eminently successful traditional Lao patron. The children

like the music television channel, cartoons, superhero shows,
space shows and karate or military shows. The hostess will
serve drinks (water or soft drinks depending on finances,
with beer for the men) and perhaps some food (watermelon,
apples, oranges, etc.) to her guests. This informal gathering
may become an impromptu party if enough guests, music and
alcohol (for men) are added.

Children, as well as adults, will fall asleep when
and where they choose.

Between Men and Women:  Courtship, Marriage and Divorce

The question of dating is becoming a major point of
contention between generations.  In Laos, dating meant going
on group outings accompanied by one's brothers and sisters.
Most Lao parents are not comfortable with the American system
-- especially for daughters.  Boys may date, but if they
want to date American style, they must find American dates.
There seems to be little problem in doing so.  This has
led to the practice of Lao boys dating American girls extensively because they can get more gratification from Americans
and the dating is less restrictive.  Since Lao males are
fairly free to do much as they please, there has been little
conflict between parents and sons.  Parental concerns that
were voiced regarding sons focused more on drinking behavior
and the feeling that the sons were not listening to and
respecting the parents as they should.  One example of a

problem caused by dating follows. Actually, the problem
evolved due to the manipulation of the Lao family by a sponsor.
In essence they lost their son. The following incident
was recounted to the researcher by the family involved and
supported by various other members of the community. The
family's sponsor planned for her daughter to marry the Lao
son. She got the girl and the son a motel room and then
told the boy's mother that he must marry the daughter or
the sponsor would see that the family was sent back to Laos.
The boy was 22 and the girl was 16. He did not want to
marry the girl, but she became pregnant so he felt obligated
to do so. His family was frightened by the woman's threats
in any case and pressured him to marry the girl. The girl
said she did not like Laotians and refused to let her husband
visit his family. The couple live with the girl's parents.
The boy's family is moving to California and is very upset
but feels that their son should stay with the girl since
he slept with her. They also feel the girl is "slow" or
deficient mentally in some way. Perhaps this is why the
woman needed to acquire a son-in-law she could control.

Lao girls are faced with waiting for a Lao boy who
is interested in a traditional courtship or with defying
parental authority. One girl who defied her father on these
matters was ostracized from the family. It is particularly difficult for the girls since they unconciously are misinterpreted by some Americans. Lao females like makeup

and even four year olds wear eyeshadow, blush, lipstick and finely styled hair to celebrations. One woman at the previously mentioned public services meeting wanted sponsors to warn the Southeast Asian girls that they might be considered the "wrong sort of girls" because of the amount of makeup worn. The researcher has noted frequent evidence of interest in the Lao girls and women by American males, so she imagines that the potential for conflict over dating is fairly great.

Most of the local single Lao men ready for marriage at this point in time still prefer a Lao mate. When the men are interested in marriage they are introduced to appropriate Lao women by friends and relatives and proceed with a basically traditional courtship of visiting. They visit the woman and her family to talk and, after a period of months, a mutual friend will approach the woman's family about the possibility of a marriage. The couple themselves have already decided that this is what both want. Assuming arrangements are agreeable with all, a traditional ceremony will be held. Most of the Lao interviewed who had married in the United States followed the traditional ceremony with a legal wedding. Only a few, at the urging of sponsors, followed it with a church wedding. Several couples in the study were not married according to the United States law, having only participated in a traditional ceremony while in camp or in the United States. If one individual (or both) has a spouse in Laos somewhere with whom they have lost contact, the couple may have only a traditional ceremony. It is important to the adult Lao of either sex to have a family, so if the old one has been torn asunder by the refugee experience, a new one is started. There are precedents for polygamy in traditional Lao society. Men who are affluent enough may take a second wife (LeBar and Suddard, 1967). The first wife is the mia luan and the second is the mia noy. Most of the Columbus refugees, being from a poorer, rural background, did not participate in this system in Laos, but it was still a cultural alternative. Only one example of a Lao man coming to Columbus with both a mia noy and mia luan was known to the interpreter for this project. In this case the man committed a terrible faux pas for which he paid dearly. The first wife is always to get more respect and yet this man told officials that his mia luan and their children were his widowed sister and her children. He claimed his mia noy as his wife. This offended and angered his mia luan. The American sponsor for the family was an older gentleman who took a liking to the "widowed sister" and eventually proposed to her. She accepted and the man lost his wife and children to the American sponsor. According to Visa the Lao women all found this amusing and felt the man got what he deserved for not showing proper respect to his first wife. The Lao are aware that Americans feel one should be monogamous and will say that they have divorced a spouse left in Laos when, in reality, no formal or informal severance of the union has occurred. Circumstances have merely conspired to keep them apart.

Divorce does occur in Laos and in the Columbus Lao community. Although the researcher gathered no statistics specifically on this, the feeling of the community members was that the rate of divorce and reasons for divorce remained about the same in Columbus as they had been in Laos. One reason for the ease of divorce in Columbus is that generally individuals (male or female) have access to a network of friends and/or relatives who can assist the party who wishes to leave. The reasons for divorce can be economic (usually the husband is seen as an ineffective provider); unfaithfulness (for men or women, although this is more apt to be of concern in a wife than in a husband); interference from relatives; or no-fault (the people just do not get along with each other). A good example of interference by relatives can be seen in the following incident. A woman had an abortion and her husband approved of it. Her mother-in-law had never liked the wife and took this matter as an important issue. She forced her son to send his wife away even though the husband and wife both say they love each other and would rather still be married. No stigma is attached to divorce and the parties are free to get back together and separate several times (quite a few couples have had on again, off again relationships).

Local Lao women characterized the ideal man as liking to work and to provide for the family. Women should stay home and men should not have to do the housework. From the researcher's observations, men do not assist much with the housework even if they are unemployed and the wife works. Men should be polite and quiet and strong. Traditionally men are five or more years older than the wife, although, as in other matters, personal preference may override this convention. The older age of the male helps to insure a more harmonious marriage because the husband will be wiser and so be respected by his wife.

Local men characterize the ideal woman as being pretty and polite. She should stay home and cook, do housework, and help the children. While women should dress nicely, they should not wear too much makeup. The men do not like women who "talk too much or gossip or are running around in other people's business instead of staying home".

Overt relationships between husband and wife are to be controlled, polite, respectful and somewhat distant. Physical and verbal interaction is minimal. At gatherings the men sit together and play cards or watch television and talk in one area while the women sit and prepare food and talk in another. The major interaction is nonverbal and consists of women bringing food or drink to the men. The men bring out the whiskey and pass it around themselves, but most of the other food and drink is placed in front

of the group of men or in front of individuals by the women.
It is much the situation that exists between adults and
children.   In mixed groups interaction between the sexes
is minimal.   One stoops to avoid walking upright in front
of another.   Eye contact is frequently indirect and politeness
and respect are maximized.   In all-female gatherings, however,
the rules change:   the talk is noisier, people are not as
concientious of stooping when walking in front of others,
most eye contact is direct, and things are more relaxed
in general.   The women joke and laugh and complain about
their husbands.   Most complaints involve laziness.   The
women joke about doing girlish things again (like being
in a beauty contest or dating).   Although physical interaction
in public is taboo between sexes, women habitually greet
each other with a hug and there is frequent tactile interaction.   Women frequently style each other's hair, put makeup
on a friend and otherwise groom each other.   In many ways
it seems that the bond between women is stronger than that
between a woman and her husband -- it is certainly more
openly affectionate and interactive.

Pregnancy and Children

        There is a growing tendency for the Lao women in Columbus
to limit offspring out of economic concerns.   Birth control
is accepted with many women using intrauterine devices or
diaphragms.   Birth control was not practiced to any great

extent in Laos, at least by the women in this study. Many women complained about weakness, tiredness and nausea while using birth control, perhaps due to some sense of guilt. Some of the women have had abortions since coming to the United States. Most told their husbands and it seemed to be accepted. The reason given by the women for the abortion is always economic: e.g. "We cannot afford more children", "Children are expensive here", "I need to work". Yet the women also are reluctant to talk about abortion and say they wonder whether the baby was a boy or girl. Whether this is a common cross-cultural reaction or based in Lao culture is beyond the scope of this research. Nonetheless the use of contraceptives and abortions have had some effect on traditional attitudes toward ideal family size -- especially in conjunction with new economic realities.

The data collected here are not sufficient to generate conclusions, but it does show some indications that pregnancy is regarded as a time of illness by the woman. Several of the women in the study talked about how sick they were through their entire pregnancies and two said they spent most of each pregnancy in the hospital. The researcher constantly received comments from the Lao women about how lucky she was to be so strong and to not have problems with her own pregnancy.

Traditionally childbirth took place in the home with the help of female relatives and, perhaps, a midwife. After birth the mother was placed on a hot bed and cleansed. She might be treated with the hot bed and special foods for a varying length of time, by her preference. A few of the women had births in clinics or hospitals. Those who had children in camp, also used a hospital with one exception. This woman joked that the baby came so fast there was not time to go anywhere. Since coming to the United States, births have consistently taken place in hospitals. Women who have experienced both a hospital/clinic birth and a home birth all preferred the home birth. After the birth at home, friends are all around and people talk and visit and have fun. However, hospitals have not presented any particular problems for the Lao women. Most of the women have been going to a doctor or clinic throughout their pregnancy. They are accompanied by social service agents, sponsors, or friends. Usually the husband (and a bilingual companion if the husband does not speak English) accompanies the woman to the hospital for birth, but does not attend the birth itself. Communication is largely through nonverbal means and the women are at the mercy of hospital policy and preference. The women seem to trust the doctors to provide adequate care and -- while one could hardly characterize the situation as nonstressful - seem at no real disadvantage when compared to other pregnant women.

One woman had a great deal of difficulty in achieving a successful birth. Three pregnancies resulted in a baby

being born that was stillborn or that died within a day
or two. The woman finally went to a religious curing specialist
who told her there was a snake inside her that was killing
her babies. He treated her during the time of *wan sin* (holy
days). She became pregnant again. This time she gave birth
in a refugee camp in the Philippines and the child lived.
A skeptic might suggest that the differing environment sur-
rounding the birth (a clinic with medical personnel versus
a home birth attended by relatives) might have influenced
the outcome. The woman and the community give full credit
to the specialist. As further proof of the efficacy of
the cure, the woman offers the success of her subsequent
pregnancy in the United States.

Food:  More Than A Meal

The importance of food to the Lao is best symbolized
by the family who kept their refrigerator in the living
room.  To the Lao refugees, food means hospitality, and
hospitality means being Lao. Whenever anyone comes to one's
house, one must offer hospitality -- i.e. food or drink.
What is offered depends on the relationship between visitor
and host, and the economic position of the host. A glass
of water is perfectly acceptable if that is all the host
can afford. A very few of the younger couples do not seem
to honor this tradition as fully as they should, but Visa
explains this by saying that the Lao realize Americans are

different and do not give each other presents so some Lao think it is not so important to give hospitality here in the United States. Visa feels this is not a good idea. For the Lao it is important to offer hospitality to all. If one is a patron one owes this kindness to clients by virtue of showing generosity. If one is a client, one owes this kindness to the patron and people associated with the patron by virtue of showing loyalty. In addition to food, one may be expected to extend lodgings or money. The Lao extend their hospitality to non-Lao as well. During one interview a black woman came to the family's door and said she was a neighbor. She then asked to borrow the family's vacuum cleaner. Without hesitation, the woman gave it to her. After the neighbor had left, the researcher asked who she was and where she lived. No one in the family had seen her before.

In addition to its uses for hospitality, food and eating are seen as enjoyable pastimes. Food preparation is usually a cooperative task and, as previously mentioned, involves joking and gossip. Meals are communal -- at least within gender and age groups. If a group of people is present, adult males usually eat together, as do adult females and children of both sexes. Within the family, or with small groups, no division will necessarily take place. While there may be individual servings of some foods, the norm is for food to be served on communal plates and shared with all present. The Lao love food and no one is under compunction to hold back. While Lao women are expected to try to be slender, no one pretends to be full when they are not or says they are on a diet and cannot eat. Eating is fun.

Food is also seen as a response to emotional trauma. Babies who fuss, children who are unhappy and adults who are sad, all are offered food. Going along with the idea of respect and tolerance for children, the Lao will not refuse a child food. If they ask for it, they will get it. Giving children treats is a favorite occurrence for adults.

It is not just the host who provides food. Visitors frequently bring food when they come to visit. While there is no set rule for how often this is done, expectations are that frequent visitors will bring something every second or third visit; infrequent visitors may be expected to bring something every time. Again, the nature of the gift depends on the relationship of the people and the economics involved. Typical presents include fruit (apples, bananas, watermelons, strawberries) and beer. Milk, cheese and even White Castle hamburgers are also given. Presents brought for children are usually fruit, candy or gum.

The staple foods have remained the same in Columbus as they were in Laos. Sticky rice is always available, stored in baskets. Meats used include chicken, pork, sausage, and beef. Fish is also favored. Rice noodles in various dimensions are used and vegetables include many varieties (e.g. lettuce, onion, carrots, bean sprouts and vegetables Americans lump under "Chinese vegetables"). Seasonings vary widely but frequently used are coconut (and its milk), hot peppers, garlic, and the ever-present fish sauce (made from anchovies primarily). Much food shopping is done at Chinese, Cambodian, Thai or Lao markets. Columbus refugees are fortunate to have a number of local stores which provide otherwise hard to find ingredients. A few of the luckier Lao actually have room to have a garden by their apartment and tend their plants carefully. Seeds and starting plants are traded and brought to Columbus from areas with more accommodating climates (such as Florida). Most local Lao do not have access to a garden though.

In addition to these more traditional foods the Lao have incorporated a variety of American foods into their diet -- although for the most these are occasional supplements rather than everyday food. Fast foods are very popular. Pizza, hamburgers and hot dogs head the list. Particularly favored are the White Castle hamburgers (called "hamburger noy") which are heavily flavored with onion. Most Lao can also make hamburgers and hot dogs at home, but add a lot of seasonings to make them spicier. For example at a party a fellow graduate student was grilling hamburgers for a Lao group. Some of the girls approached him and asked him to join them in a game of water volleyball. One of the

women immediately stepped up to the grill. After the graduate
student was a discreet distance away, she smiled and said
"good, now we can make them right". She proceeded to add
large wedges of onion and peppers to the meat as she formed
the patties. The patties were heavily salted before being
put on the grill. The girls had deliberately lured the
cook away so that the woman could take over without offending
him. Most of the Lao could not yet make pizza at the time
of this study, but the skill was progressing fairly quickly
throughout the community since pizza is a favored food and
is expensive to buy.

Although canned soup is sometimes used, most Lao women
simply make their own using chicken broth and adding pieces
of chicken, green onion and small "Chinese" noodles. The
canned soups are considered rather bland.

Breakfast cereals are extremely popular with the children
as is anything else sugary and sweet. The adults do not
care for the very sweet foods and use fruits or custards
as desserts, but the children have embraced American junk
food of all types. Given the Lao attitude of laissez—faire
regarding children and food, American dentists have probably
hit a gold mine!

Commonly used beverages are a mixture of old and new.
The Lao do not drink with a meal, but regard the two as
separate activities. Water and tea (hot or cold) are frequently
drunk as are fruit juices. No sugar or milk is added to

the tea, and they prefer the green tea types. Fruit juices, like their solid counterparts, are considered more of a sweet snack than a beverage. Soft drinks, however, are a big hit and any kind will do. A few of the Lao have deliberately attempted to introduce milk, hot chocolate, and coffee as beverages since they know these are used frequently by Americans.

It is probable that the Lao have a high frequency of lactase deficiency. The Lao are closely related to Thai, as previously mentioned, and the Thai have a very high frequency of lactase deficiency[2]. This deficiency impedes the ability to digest milk sugar (lactose). Any quantity of lactose can cause side effects such as diarrhea. Nonetheless, responding to American ideas that "milk is a natural"[3] most Lao families initially tried to introduce milk into the children's diets. Most of the children rejected it and the matter was dropped. A few of the more acculturated Lao adults insist on having hot chocolate on a cold night, in spite of the consequences. Similarly most Lao adults sincerely prefer tea to coffee, but those in the position of important patrons frequently drink coffee, at least when Americans are present. Food and drink, then may also be seen as a symbol of acculturation or communication between Lao leaders and American contacts.

The young children eagerly embrace the American foods. They are served them at school and they like junk food because

it is sweet and/or salty. Some even reject traditional
foods. Many women told the researcher that their young
children would not eat Lao food, but complained saying,
"not that stuff again, I want hamburger". Older children
and teens like both American food and Lao food which they
have had most of their lives. Because the children do like
American food, some of the women have attended a nutrition
class given by a local agency. There they learn how to
make pizza, peanut butter and jelly sandwiches, macaroni
and cheese, and hamburgers among other American fare. Dietary
advice is also offered. Attendance is variable and most
favored recipes are passed throughout the community via
Lao networks. There is some amusement expressed at the
thought that the teacher thinks the Lao adults would ever
really want to eat like Americans. It is mostly for the
children that Lao women learn to cook Ameican foods. The
classes are beneficial for showing the Lao the mechanics
of shopping and reading labels. The classes also concentrate
on storage advice -- important because most Lao have not
had to deal with this before: most food was obtained as
needed, and, as mentioned before, many are having their
first contact with electricity and, hence, refrigeration.
The nutrition counselors, as are all available Americans,
are also used to decode utility bills and other English
correspondence. Not surprisingly it is the adults who are
least accepting of American food although everybody seems

to like pizza and Pepsi. Men who work expect their wives
to pack a lunch, or they try to return home at noon, so
that they do not have to eat American food.


Networks and Lao Women:  Cohesive Factors in a Factionalized
Community.

In traditional Lao society, the nuclear family would
be firmly ensconced in the extended uxori-parentilocal family
which, in turn, would be ensconced in the larger concerns
of friends and relatives who make up a village. Movement
to urban areas or movement due to government employment
had already disrupted this system within Laos for a few
of the families studied. Most did come directly from this
system to the United States -- and they came without parents
or siblings, stripped overnight of the extended family.
Women, more than men, seen to feel this loss. This is hardly
surprising since it is usually their family of birth which
made up the household group they left. As Visa put it "when
I had my parents, I was ok. There were no problems. Now
they are gone (in Laos) and I am the one who is lost".
A woman could turn to sisters for help with household duties
and to parents for security. Child care was given automatically. There were always friendly hands to make a task
easier and enjoyable. In America, the women are faced with
the same responsibilities and a lack of familiarity with
methods of meeting these responsibilities. Worst of all,
they are alone. Their mothers and sisters are gone. The

women sill must cope with the tasks of child care, food preparation, housework, managing finances, and maintaining the health and identity of the Lao family. In addition to these traditional responsibilities many of the women work at full or part time jobs. This means delegating traditional duties to others and a new responsibility of providing or contributing financial support for the family. Actually many women in Laos participate in small businesses (sewing or trading) to bring in money so this last responsibility is not entirely new[4]. However the unemployment of the men in the face of the wife's employment is new.

The use of American patrons (be these public assistance programs or institutions such as churches) is one answer to meeting responsibilities -- particularly those of an economic nature. Public assistance programs are utilized to get needed money, food and health care. Churches and American sponsors may also supply food and money as well as leads to jobs. Some churches assist with the day care needs of working Lao mothers. Mothers are ambivalent in regards to the use of American day care systems. Some, particularly younger mothers, see it as a chance for the children to learn about Americans. Most mothers prefer for their children to stay in the care of a Lao friend since they are perceived as undeniably trustworthy and better able to understand the child's needs. School age children are not seen as needing supervision and are expected to

take care of themselves. This Lao attitude has caused some
problems with local authorities who, from an American point
of view, regard six year olds as unable to care for themselves
and perceive this as child neglect. Because of this women
are more careful about leaving children ostensibly under
a neighbor's care (although the reality of minimal supervision
continues). No Lao woman expects payment for taking care
of another's children. Children are a pleasure and anyone
who is not working is happy to open her home to other children.
Given the fact that these children are cared for mostly
by their peers, not the woman, a charge would seem out of
line -- there is little added burden. The fact that the
children eat someone else's food is not considered. If
a woman is watching one's children, she will have other
ties to one as well and, during the course of visiting and
communal meals, a balance of exchange will be approximated.
The economic pattern in most Lao exchanges is one of generalized
reciprocity. No tally of gifts and receipts is kept, but
an approximate balance of exchange is maintained. The intimacy
of a relationship is reflected in the frequency of exchange,
the personal nature of the gift and the value of the exchange
rather than in the type of exchange. Increasing intimacy
leads to increasing frequency of exchange, greater personal-
ization of the gift and exchange of more highly valued commodities or services.

Because Lao women are so oriented to communal tasks
they have sought, successfully, to create new networks to
replace those of extended family and friends lost 'in the
refugee experience. Americans do not really enter these
networks for any stable period of time in most cases. Most
Americans that enter the network do so as patrons. Even
if an American woman marries a Lao man, she is unlikely
to be included in the community in any real sense. After
all, she has no need of the Lao networks, she has her own
contacts and systems for living -- this is her society.
Some Americans may be inducted as fictive kin, but even
then their role is actually more one of patronage than relative. Visa, for example, says that her American sponsors
are like parents to her in this country. Still they serve
mainly as a source of information on American expectations
and customs, rather than in any true kinship role. The
American most fully inducted into Lao society in the local
community was a young boy. The boy was experiencing difficulties at home, became friends with some of the Lao children
and was invited to the children's homes. He enjoyed the
feeling of welcome that he found there and essentially started
living with several of the Lao families. The families told
the researcher that the boy spoke "just like a Lao. And
he likes our food too". At the nucleus of all Lao networks
is the idea that the Lao "help each other". This phrase
was often repeated to the researcher. It was also given

as a reason for secondary migration to Columbus several
times -- i.e. "the Lao in Columbus, really help each other".
Van Esterik (1983:13) also mentions the use of this phrase
in the community he studied.

For men this help frequently revolves around patron-client
systems and as a result male relationships may cause factionalism rather than community.  For example, the Lao community
is fortunate in that there are Lao workers in most major
agencies who can assist members of the local community.
There are Lao contacts in the Department of Health, Department
of Welfare, Job Services, and Resettlement Offices.  There
are also Lao who serve as teacher's aides for the Columbus
Public School System.  These workers are also all important
Lao patrons and are also patrons of the same faction with
one exception.  Visa's husband is associated with a rival
faction, but Visa serves as a contact between the Lao community
and the larger Columbus community.  That these men are of
the same faction makes sense.  Americans tend to depend
on the advice of a particularly well-known Lao patron for
information regarding who is dependable and who should be
hired.  The patron, of course, backs his own clients.  The
researcher constantly heard charges from people that patrons
would give preferential treatment to their own clients,
charge for free services if a person was not associated
with the patron, or even deprive one of benefits if one
did not go through the patrons to obtain these benefits.

For example, the patron in Job Services was accused of selling jobs and of getting people fired who did not get jobs through his office. He supposedly accomplished this by telling employers the people were unreliable and offering them better workers. Since there is a limited pool of employers who hire most Lao workers and these employers do work with this patron, the veracity of the charges is possible -- they have not been substantiated in any way however. Certainly these kind of networks do not cement community relationships.

Even so, one can use these patron-client networks as a good source of income. Several of the local Lao men have started trading goods from other cities to Columbus (or vice versa), or selling used cars or insurance. These men, again, are important patrons or patrons on the rise. Any member of the community, other than an opposing patron or the very close associates of an opposing patron, will take advantage of the chance to deal with someone they know and who speaks their own language.

The Lao women, on the other hand, create networks for accomplishing every day tasks communally. As such, these networks do not focus on patron-client relationships, nor on power, nor on competition. Instead they focus on cooperation. All child care whether the mother works or not may be handled communally with the peer group being sovereign in most matters. Any Lao women in the vicinity, however, may be expected to give food, drink or aid to the group when it is needed or desired. Household chores, shopping and food preparation are done communally if possible. The Lao have largely concentrated in certain apartment complexes due to a need for low-income housing, but also out of a desire for easy access to other Lao. This is even more important for the women than for the men since most men drive and have access to a car. Most women do not drive, and even if they did, most families have only one car which the man controls. The few women who do not live near other Lao are those who lament their loneliness the most and who actively seek to establish contact with their non-Lao neighbors since no Lao are available.

How are members of this communal group chosen? If one were in Laos, one's social network would include a woman's family of birth, her family by marriage, other relatives, fictive kin and friends who share common age and interests[5]. Fictive kinship terminology can signify either respect or liking. That is, one must call a slightly older individual whom one respects "pa" or "loong"[6]. In this case, use of the kin term denotes respect rather than a feeling of kinship. On the other hand, calling someone "aye" (older brother) or "yaye" (older sister) acknowledges an age difference, but also indicates more affection. The Lao have lots of "cousins". That is, if close friends are gathered and an

American asks who the people are, the Lao (man or woman) usually replies that they are "cousins".

Basically the same factors govern selection of associates in the United States as in Laos. If one is lucky enough to have relatives in the United States they will form the core of one's group. Proximity is a factor, particularly for the women who lack access to transportation. That is, one finds it convenient to interact with one's neighbors. In some ways proximity has replaced kinship in determining everyday interaction. One's neighbors become like one's sisters. Geographical distance should not be overrated as an obstacle to interaction, though. The Lao are used to traveling long distances for business or pleasure in their native communities and none of the Lao in Columbus are isolated from any other as far as occasional visits go by geographical distance alone. Political factionalism and traditionally based discrimination (e.g. against Lao-Chinese) does produce some isolation. It does, however, affect daily interaction of women since they have limited access to modes of transportation. Since consanguineal and affinal kin have been dispersed by the refugee experience, there is a tendency for the women to seek replacements among other refugees and to accord these replacements with kin status -- a true example of fictive kinship. Coming from the same area of Laos also contributes to mutual compatibility to some degree as different areas vary in speech, food styles

and style of music. This factor is not of major importance
in the Columbus community however. Van Esterik (1983) found
clear community divisions due to area of origin in Laos.
This is not the case in Columbus. But Columbus does not
have major patrons from different provinces either, nor
one group of patrons associated with previous administrative
(civil) positions and another previously associated with
the military as did Van Esterik's community. Coming from
the same area of Laos can help a relationship, but coming
from different areas does not seem to impede a relationship.

In characteristic Lao style, respecting the individual,
personal preference is an important factor in selecting
networks. People who share common interests or skills,
who are of similiar age and temperament, choose to associate
frequently with each other. While propriety requires certain
perfunctory interaction between kin, the Lao may not go
beyond this propriety into real friendship if they do not
like the individual. The intensity of interaction is determined
foremost by the degree of liking involved.

These networks form the basis of various informal cooper-
atives which operate throughout the community. For example,
several women habitually travel to Akron (driven by one
of the few women who drives and whose family has two cars)
in order to buy chickens directly from farmers at wholesale
prices. They bring these back and distribute them, via
the female networks, to the entire community. One woman

involved in this told the researcher that one time she had
gone to a local market and had seen chickens there. The
sign said "40 cents" and she thought "chickens for 40 cents,
I'll get a lot". She gathered an armful of chickens and
took them to a clerk only to be confronted with an astronomical
bill. The clerk explained to the shocked woman that the
forty cents meant forty cents a pound, not per chicken.
She laughed and said "Now, I know better, so I can help
my friends".

Women will also arrange for some men (husbands, brothers,
etc.) to purchase a cow from a farmer and butcher it. The
women arrange the venture by paying in shares (usually around
$25.00 per family) until a sufficient amount is collected.
The meat obtained is then distributed to the participating
women. Even in wage work, women evidence a communal nature.
Many women work together as seamtresses and, rather than
associating with non-Lao co-workers, talk and eat together
while at work.

Men's supplemental economic activities, on the other
hand, are more individually oriented. One favorite supplemental
activity is collecting worms. This activity has even drawn
other Lao refugees to the Columbus area. While a group
of men may go worm collecting together, once they arrive
at the location, each is on his own. Women do not usually
go since they must watch young children and so would be
less productive. Each person collects worms and keeps them

separate from all others. Each individual sells his own worms and keeps the money. This is true even of children who participate. They will be expected to give some money to a grandparent if one is present7, but may keep the rest.

Women's networks cross cut the male political factions. The wife of one patron may socialize regularly with the wife of a rival patron. It is the men who will not. Occasionally the factionalism will disrupt a female cooperative venture. At one point the women of several families in an apartment complex were interested in having a cooperative garden. A site about two miles distant (easy walking distance for Lao) was located, but then the plans stopped and eventually were dropped. Two patrons of rival factions lived in the complex and when the garden seemed a potenial reality they decided that someone would have to take credit for such an important contribution. Although the women would do most of the work, it is the men, as household heads, that needed to agree to the garden. Instead of agreeing , members of rival factions became embroiled in debate over the division of the plots and who should approach the owner of the proposed site. The garden plan was lost in a quagmire of detail.

Generally the women's networks continue in spite of political factionalism. These networks are used for information as well. News of jobs or assistance programs are passed through the community and to other communities by means of them. Sources of potential mates, traditional curing specialists and other rare commodities are passed as well. These networks give refugees mobility since one can always find a relative or "cousin" to live with upon moving to a new community. The "cousin" may not have direct acquaintance with the family, but a friend of a friend is always welcome. Upon the arrival of a new family, whether they are locally sponsored by Americans or if they have migrated on their own to Columbus, the Lao community takes over. Through female networks the family is provided with clothes and food and generally welcomed to the community. Van Esterik (1983) credits the networks which allow mobility to patron-client relationships. While some is undoubtedly due to these, at least locally, hospitality is usually offered in deference to some previous connection in Laos or because of perceived relationship due to common association with a peer -- not in deference to one's patron (who is not a peer, but is in a superior power position). This previous connection does not have to be direct. Visa's husband has a large circle of friends who either know his father, or whose fathers knew his father. Access to public assistance, however, does frequently follow a patron-client pattern.

Women, then, serve to integrate a community that may otherwise be fragmented by political factionalism. Males are to some degree peripheral to the community's day to day life in Laos and continue to be so in the United States. That is, in Laos a man, upon marriage, enters his wife's family and social network. Frequently his occuption (merchant, soldier, government worker) takes him from his home for prolonged periods of time. Men participate extensively in leadership roles and in networks that lead to factionalism rather than to unity. It is women and their social ties that form the glue that holds the fabric of the community together. It is men's affinal ties to the women's networks that offers stability and constancy amidst the factionalism of their political framework. The women's networks help to draw new people into the community as well and to provide for the needs that public assistance programs do not even recognize: access to traditional foods, clothes and to the networks that make day to day living bearable and friendly instead of harsh and lonely.

Women also are the source and protectors of tradition. If Lao find identity through helping each other as Van Esterik (1983) claims, then surely Lao women form the core of this identity. In every aspect of their daily lives they are constantly involved in generalized reciprocity. They are the ones who provide the traditional accoutrements of hospitality -- the food, the drink, the warmth of welcome. The women are the ones who encourage communal activities and the traditional caretaking and nurturing attitudes on the part of older children toward younger children. While this leaves opportunity for a tremendous generation gap as the children are pulled more and more into American society by their American peers, it also fosters some very traditional Lao values such as dependence upon and interaction with peers. In addition, the children have proven remarkably adept at cultural switching, going from a passable (albeit somewhat tentative) American at school to the good Lao child at home.

Lastly it is the Lao women who maintain a traditional Lao home into which men may retreat. They wear Lao clothing at home, serve Lao food and promote respect and self-control in their children. Although the women are gaining responsibility in some families by being the sole wage earner, this has not markedly influenced family structure at this point. The men do not like the women working when the men are not; but, other than this point of pride, little changes. Men have not taken over women's duties, but rather women have allocated these duties in a traditional fashion to other women (or to American institutions such as daycare). Women have always controlled the purse strings (Hoskins, 1976, discusses this in Vietnamese culture; Potter, 1977, in Thai) so the source of the money is of little importance. There is no real increase in independence due to income, since the income is perceived as family, rather than individual, property[8] and the true Lao independence has always resided in an extensive personal social network rather than in money anyway. Because of the importance of women in establishing these networks and in providing for the family and maintaining

the traditions of Laos in the home, women are the heart
of the family. The Lao, themselves, recognize this and
both men and women say that women are the "strongest part
of the family"9. Indeed it seems clear that in women and
in their roles resides the kernal of Lao identity. The
data on Lao women substantiates the idea of low cultural
status (based in Buddhism) and high structural status.
The importance of female networks, women's roles, entrepreneurial activities, affinal ties and female ultimogeniture
are examples supporting this idea.

# CHAPTER SIX

## FUTURE ADDITIONS

### Summation

The research problem has been to investigate the roles of women in the local Lao community and the strategies which have been employed to cope with the new environment in which these women find themselves. These topics were investigated by means of participant observation and a series of open-ended interviews within the local Lao community. An interpreter was used. The interpreter was usually female. A male interpreter did assist with eight of the formal interviews.

The Lao women have retained their traditional roles to a large degree. Women are seen as the backbone of the family. They must provide food, clothing, housekeeping services and childcare duties to the family. They are responsible for the finances. They also form the core of the community by providing the social networks which lead to communal life and the necessary offerings of hospitality. It is primarily the strategies which are used to fulfill these roles that have altered. Women are involved with wage labor, public assistance programs, American patrons,

American churches and the American educational system.
The basic strategy remains the same however: invest in
extensive social relationships. The security of the farm
and of the extended family is gone, so substitutions must
be made for these. Assistance programs provide a basis
for life (although fostering some value conflicts) and
friendships based on geographic proximity, common area
of origin within Laos, and personal preference have been
expanded to include functions previously fulfilled only
by family. Part of the Lao cultural system is its inherent
flexibility of interpersonal relationships and this flexibility
has proven most adaptive in the context of the refugee
situation.

A secondary concern has been the nature of culture
contact between the Lao community and the host society.
Most conjunctive relations between the Lao and their hosts
are through multilingual males who serve in an official
capacity (employed by an agency which assists refugees
or by mutual assistance associations M.A.A.'s) as well
as in an unofficial capacity of community leadership.
The cultural contact is largely filtered through these
individuals although all Lao are in contact with American
culture to some degree. Due to the nature of the contact
situation one might expect the Lao to be overwhelmed and
subjected to strong assimilative pressures. That is, the
Lao culture is fairly flexible and has few boundary maintaining

mechanisms. Nonetheless, there is little evidence for assimilation at this point. Factors encouraging continued autonomy
of the Lao include the open nature of the host society,
the effectiveness of Lao self-correcting mechanisms, the
perception of many adult Lao of themselves as visitors
rather than as citizens-to-be, and, perhaps most importantly,
the degree of cultural difference between the host culture
and the Lao.

At this point one finds a clearly defined Lao community
with traditional values, food choices, clothing and language.
Traditional religious beliefs and prestige/leadership systems
continue. It is too early to say if this is a condition
of "stabilized pluralism" (Social Science Research Council
Seminar, 1954). This incident of acculturation is still
at its beginning and, at this time, a see-saw between pluralism
and assimilation with ultimate retention of a degree of
pluralism seems likely (as suggested by Newman, 1973, for
physically different ethnic groups in America).

Some Implications of This Research:

Previous governmental policies have favored a dispersement
of refugees within the host country so that financial burdens
involved in supporting resettlement would be spread more
evenly over a number of different cities. This policy
is particularly detrimental to the Lao since the success
of everyday living is so dependent upon having adequate

social networks and these networks can only be filled adequately by Lao. So far the Lao have successfully overcome this obstacle through secondary migration. It would seem wise to introduce new refugees into areas where a strong link to the existing network could be found. The local refugee community would be able to assist the new refugees by helping them find traditional resources; introducing them to local patrons who can get them to public assistance programs; and fitting them into the local support networks. The financial burden to the host city would be somewhat mitigated by the initial direct aid offered by the community and the continuing support received from community members. The implication for resettlement in general is that an attempt should be made by agency personnel to familiarize themselves with traditional coping strategies and to utilize the traditional orientation of the group, be it communal, individualistic, or other.

Basically the researcher agrees with the suggestions proposed by Van Esterik (1983:47) to make programs more accessible to the Lao. These suggestions follow:

1) Continue English language training even when a client is employed and find ways of adjusting times and schedules to include all Lao adults.

2) Discover ways to make vocational training programs accessible to refugees with minimal educational backgrounds.

3) Encourage the development of Lao administered Mutual Assistance Associations which develop a full spectrum of services in conjunction with a community-based organization.

4) Increase orientation and social adjustment services for Lao refugees.

5) Develop counseling skills among educated Lao who can advise programs across the nation.

6) Begin a program that provides support services to young Lao including those in families and attending high school.

The thrust of these policy suggestions is to bring the Lao into a very complex society with the skills they need to survive and adapt. A part of this adjustment includes the building upon already existing network relations to build associations that can themselves adjust to an American cultural context.

Scudder and Colson (1982:287) also raise several policy implications based on current knowledge of the involuntary migration and resettlement process. Two are particularly relevant to the Lao group:

In most programs . . . far too much emphasis is placed on the provision of housing and far too little on the generation of economic opportunities for the relocatees. Such economic planning as is carried out, almost without exception, relates to the male head of household to the exclusion of women and children. In this regard relocation often weakens the domestic unit as a decision-making and production unit contrary to the stated intentions of the planners.

In relocation communities planners need to pay far more attention to community formation. Far too much emphasis is now being placed on the household head as opposed to the household and the community.

It seems to the researcher that most policy makers have been overlooking the utility of Lao women in promoting programs. Almost all contact has been with bilingual male patrons, but these patrons belong to networks that are highly factionalized. If one were to make programs directly accessible to the women and suitable to their needs, the programs might receive better support from the community. For example, English lessons have been primarily offered in the evenings at locations which necessitate use of a car or other transportation for most of the Lao participants. Attendance has been on again, off again and minimal. While this research has not dealt extensively with language programs, some suggestions can be offered on the basis of the information gathered on Lao culture. Evenings are a bad time for classes because this is the time associated with visiting. Far from being simply a form of entertainment, visiting is an important aspect of establishing and maintaining those all important social networks. Further, by requiring the Lao to commute, so to speak, Americans are requiring the Lao to put a fair amount of effort into something which makes them feel uncomfortable and at which they do not particularly feel successful. When they get to class, most Lao women have problems because the teachers do not appreciate the presence of children. The women are also inconvenienced if they must leave their children at home since, according to American norms, they must find an appropriate caretaker. Most importantly, perhaps, there is no direct correlation between acquiring English speaking ability and getting a job -- the job market is not flooded with opportunities for unskilled labor. To the Lao, there

is little incentive to go beyond present economic needs,
and the English required by these is minimal. If the women
can deal with the store clerks and say "hello", most perceived
needs are satisfied. While lack of English speaking ability
is mentioned as an obstacle to incorporating Americans
into a social network, tacitly it is realized that the
cultural obstacles alone in most cases would still impede
any real integration.

How might one improve the situation? Making English
lessons available at someone's home during the day might
be a start. The women might be interested in an informal,
conversational approach to English offered in a communal
setting. Instead of demanding a formal classroom atmosphere,
learning could take place in a relaxed interactional fashion.
Children could continue their normal activities and instead
of being regarded as distractions, they might listen in
and learn, or even become a subject of conversation. The
informal atmosphere could also encourage the women to utilize
the teacher for other questions regarding Americans and
American culture. Using a young female teacher who was
able to function in somewhat of a peer relationship (as
opposed to a teacher—student relationship) would also help.
Some of these strategies would seem effective for males
as well. Males might benefit from a less formal atmosphere
and a more convenient location and time for lessons. An
older male teacher would probably be more comforting to

the Lao men -- that is, they would be learning from someone who would have greater status along traditional lines in addition to having higher status due to the particular situation. Separate male and female classes for adults seem a good idea so that conversation is more comfortable and questions of relative status do not interfere with display of knowledge. Women, for example, would not be free to show a greater linguistic skill than their husbands in mixed classes. The association of English lessons with vocational training and available jobs would provide attendance incentive for the unemployed Lao. Until English is seen as a practical tool for getting the basics of life, it may be regarded by the older Lao as merely an avenue for locating American patrons (as Van Esterik, 1983, suggests).

Likewise schools should recognize the effects of Lao culture on the interaction of the American educational system and Lao children. Parental nonparticipation should not be confused with lack of interest or concern. Rather it should be seen as a function of the world view which sees academics as the student's job alone and sees parents as nonparticipants -- especially since most also feel inadequate to offer any aid due to limited educational background and limited English speaking competency. The Lao student might, at least initially, offer a formal, reserved relationship to the American teacher due to Lao perceptions of appropriate behavior. Participation may largely consist of listening.

The reticience of a Lao student with his/her teacher may be overcome by using more of a peer group learning environment -- an environment in which Lao children may behave more freely since it involves age mates and entails few, if any, status distinctions.

Another question to be examined is that of the definition of self-sufficiency. Most refugee programs are designed with self-sufficiency as the goal. This is seen as reduced or minimal reliance on American assistance. In reality it seems this perceived self-sufficiency is not an increased ability on the part of the Lao to handle their own affairs. Rather it is a shift from American patrons who neither appreciate the loyalty a Lao client offers, nor fulfills the responsibilities and expectations a Lao has for a patron, to a Lao patron who understands the expectations of the relationship1.

Another point to be made is that many granting agencies desire that a M.A.A. show it is a community wide organization in order to obtain funds for programs. In view of the factionalism inherent in Lao leadership patterns and the association of M.A.A.'s with different Lao leaders, this is a difficult objective for the Lao community. As mentioned previously, more than one M.A.A. may exist in the community at any one time. It might be more effective to award funding on the basis of the merits of a particular program regardless of the affiliation of the sponsoring association. Although the association is affiliated with one faction; as with entertainment and services or aid, all members of the community in general (with the exception of leaders of rival factions) will gladly use a program unless prohibited (monetarily or otherwise) from so doing.

Suggestions for Continued Research

The following are areas that seem of particular interest or importance.

1) Research on the long term adjustments of Lao refugees to Columbus. Columbus has a substantial Lao community and, due to secondary migration, seems to be likely to retain one. As refugees pass from Stein's (1980) stage two to three and four, it will be interesting to see how they do or do not fit the proposed model. In even longer terms one can address the question of whether assimilation is indeed the refugee's goal. If it is, can they achieve it? If not, what is the refugee goal for fitting into their host society?

2) What is/will be the extent and nature of generational conflicts within this group? Of special interest are the young single males who are least integrated into the community, appear to be most prone to legal difficulties, and are, at least presently, mostly dating American rather than Lao women. One of the perceptions of the Lao in this study is that these young men tend to drink, drive drunk or too

fast, and fight -- this is seen as the community's main source of interaction with the American legal system. It is also these young men who are used to cause problems for rival patrons by starting fights, slashing tires, or other acts of destruction. This last characteristic is of particular significance to the stability and continuity of the community since the present research points to the integrating role of Lao women. A man who marries a nonLao may retain ties with the community -- especially his male cohorts -- but his wife will not integrate into the community, nor will their children. The man will lose access to many community resources which are obtained through women's networks (e.g. traditional food, cooperative endeavors, and family visiting with its concomitant warm social ties). It seems necessary for the survival of a separate Lao community (in any real sense) for a majority of men to marry Lao women, rather than American women.

3) The world of Lao children and their play also would be an important topic of research. A study of the adult community, while revealing something about the children, fails to truly illuminate the situation since the interaction of Lao children is, to a great extent, separate from the adult world. They are also in a somewhat stressful position. Traditionally they are taught to respect their parents and yet, due to greater exposure to American culture through school and American friends; exposure to the media (TV

in particular) and the pliability of childhood, they may be better at skills which contribute to status in the host society (i.e. English speaking ability and more education). During the present research, the author observed many times incidents that illuminated this discrepancy. Most frequently an American would be talking to Lao parents in the presence of their young children. The parents would nod politely to what was said, but the American, not trusting that comprehension was indeed achieved, would tell the child to translate for their parents. The child would smile, but not comply in spite of repeated encouragement by the American. After the American left, the parent would casually say something about the visit and the child would, indirectly, convey the visitor's message. This fits in with appropriate behavior since the parent initiated the interaction and the child was merely responding. A direct translation, as Americans urged, placed the child in the position of instructing his/her parent -- a behavior totally inappropriate to the Lao in any context.

4) An attempt was made to gather some folklore from the community, but the amount was insufficient for inclusion in the present study. The author firmly believes in the utility of folktales for illuminating cultural motifs and value systems (Dundes, 1965). A particularly fruitful and interesting source of this study is provided by the traditional dances performed by the dance troupe. This

is an integral part of traditional Lao culture and the hand movements used may even constitute a gestural language.

5) The role of television in the acculturation process and in the Lao community's perception of American society and of Americans is also an intriguing subject. Since there is so much nonselective exposure to the television (and it is not balanced by similar exposure to other mass media since most Lao cannot read English), it would be interesting to see the extent and nature of its influence. The impact of television on the acquisition of English is also an important question.

The author freely admits that the present study has initiated as many -- if not more -- questions as it has sought to answer. No apology is offered. In the author's opinion, good research is rarely conclusive. Rather good research serves to generate more, and more appropriate, questions and so to stimulate further research.

CHAPTER 1 NOTES

[1]These figures are derived from a study done of Ohio Department of Health, Refugee Services, records. The study was done by Dale Maxey, a graduate student at the Ohio State University. For a discussion of the validity of population figures and a breakdown by age and sex for the three Southeast Asian groups see Appendix One.

[2]This is when the resettlement process technically ceases. Exact definition of when this can be considered to have occurred vary. For some commonly used definitions, see Stein, 1980.

[3]For some current applications of this idea see Stein, 1980 and 1981.

[4]Some examples are found in Anthropological Quarterly, July, 1982, Volume 55, number 3. See especially the articles by Howell; Orbach and Bechwith; and Haines.

[5]Some examples are found in Anthropological Quarterly, July 1982, Volume 55, number 3. See especially the articles by Dunnigan; Scott, Jr.; and Finnan.

[6]See however, Gregory, 1984, for an interesting article dealing with the actual versus perceived accessibility to male ethnographers of data on women.

[7]See Potter, 1977; Spiro, 1977; Van Esterik, 1982.

[8]The names used for specific Lao individuals in this study are fictitious in order to protect the anonymity of the individuals. The researcher decided to specify the location of the study because this would allow readers familiar with the city to evaluate the data in the context of their own perceptions of the city. The anonymity is not for protection within the community. Most individuals referred to in the text are easily identifiable to community members because of their status or the services they provide. The anonymity is more to keep people outside of the community from invading the privacy of the community's members.

[9]The approach taken is that suggested by the Social Science Research Council Seminar (1954) on acculturation. The seminar was held in 1953.

171

[10]See Chapter 2 for further discussion of this point.

## CHAPTER 2 NOTES

[1]There are a multitude of references that could be cited – any introductory anthropology text would probably do. Some specific examples include Cohen and Eames (1982); Peacock (1980); and Honigman (1976). Malinowski (1922) also deals with the nature of anthropological research.

[2]Visa's husband was strongly associated with one political faction within the community, but the interviews that he helped with were all conducted with people who were also affiliated with that faction or were neutral to that faction. For reasons discussed under Networks in Chapter 4, Visa's affiliation did not make her any less acceptable as a cohort or as an interpreter.

[3]At the beginning of the research Mr. Thong and Visa's husband and Visa were all associated with the same main patron. By December of 1982 Mr. Thong and Visa's husband were associated with rival political factions.

## CHAPTER 3 NOTES

[1]these individuals are not necessarily biologically related to the males. The terms here indicate the social relationship between the male and the individual instead. They may be close relatives, distant relatives, friends of the male's parents, etc.

[2]for further description of these attitudes and practices see Chapter 4.

[3]several authors refer to Lao parents as leading by example or talking about good children rather than directly disciplining children. For example see Keyes (1975) and LeBar and Suddard (1967). For similar comments on a closely related Thai group see Potter (1977) and Ingersoll (1975).

## CHAPTER 4 NOTES

[1]For a very thorough discussion of the early history of Laos see Lebar and Suddard, 1967.

[2]Most of this summary comes from LeBar and Suddard, 1967.

[3]For the exact figures dealing with birth place, previous occupation in Laos, educational background, occupation in the United States and other demographic information, please see Chapter 3.

[4]Lebar and Suddard (1967) characterize the Lao as fun-loving but inherently practical and realistic.

[5]All quotes in this chapter unless specifically denoted otherwise, are from interviews or personal conversations with members of the Lao community. In some cases a represent-ative quote has been picked from a number of specific responses indicating a common response to a question, problem or issue.

[6]An oft repeated saying from conversations and interviews with the Lao — do you suppose they've seen the movie?

[7]Van Esterik (1983) also mentions this conflict avoidance and the dilemma it produces for most Americans.

[8]For parallel discussion of Lao factionalism see Van Esterik, (1983).

[9]This particular BaSi was chosen for description partially for this reason. Several BaSi were given to show Americans Lao customs -- these were somewhat shorter and less personal.

[10]Information on the Laotian educational system came from Lebar and Suddard, 1967 and from members of the Lao community in Columbus.

[11]The local Lao use the word "Kroger" to denote any large supermarket.

## CHAPTER 5 NOTES

[1]See Bourguignon 1980 for discussion.

[2]Lasker and Tyzzer, 1982, specifically deals with the Thai who are 99% lactase deficient.

[3]A commercial slogan on television, sponsored by dairy associations.

[4]For a discussion of this aspect of Lao traditional society see Kirsch, 1984.

[5]For a thorough description of a similar Thai village, see Potter, 1977.

[6]"pa" is used for father's older sister, mother's older sister, father's older brother's wife, mother's older brother's wife and mother's brother's daughter. "Loong" is used for the male counterparts of the above.

[7]This is in keeping with tradition. See Potter, 1977.

[8]See also Luong, 1984.

[9]This phrase was used several times in describing the role of women in the Lao culture. Hoskins (1976) echoes this sentiment for Vietnamese women.

## CHAPTER 6 NOTES

[1]Van Esterik (1983) deals with this question in some detail.

# APPENDIX ONE

## POPULATION ESTIMATES

The following figures were obtained by a study of Ohio Department of Health, Refugee Service, records. This agency is responsible for providing health screening and other services to refugee families who are sent to Ohio for resettlement. The figures include documented in and out secondary-migration, but do not offer any way of considering undocumented in and out secondary-migration -- that is movement where people have not notified the agency. There is no way of knowing the extent of this movement, but information obtained in interviews indicate that, for the Lao at least, it may be fairly great. In addition several individuals may maintain residences in more than one city due to work or educational requirements, or simply personal preference. The figures in these records also do not necessarily account for offspring born after initial resettlement. The records utilized covered the period of time from October, 1980 to June of 1984. No distinction is made in the records between the Lao and H'mong of Laos. Age and sex information were not available for fifty eight people who are included in the total figures.

Table One lists the health department figures for each of the three Southeast Asian groups. Tables Two and Three compare figures on the Laotian population to the numbers of individuals interviewed.

TABLE 1

Refugee Demographics

| Age | Laos Female | Male | Cambodia Female | Male | Vietnam Female | Male |
|---|---|---|---|---|---|---|
| 1 - 4 | 13 | 20 | 37 | 47 | 2 | 3 |
| 5 - 9 | 35 | 18 | 36 | 37 | 8 | 9 |
| 10 - 14 | 18 | 25 | 43 | 43 | 13 | 20 |
| 15 - 19 | 19 | 15 | 36 | 37 | 3 | 23 |
| 20 - 24 | 14 | 36 | 30 | 27 | 7 | 21 |
| 25 - 29 | 17 | 15 | 33 | 26 | 6 | 17 |
| 30 - 34 | 9 | 11 | 30 | 30 | 9 | 7 |
| 35 - 39 | 13 | 14 | 14 | 16 | 9 | 11 |
| 40 - 44 | 4 | 12 | 15 | 10 | 5 | 6 |
| 45 - 49 | 6 | 2 | 10 | 14 | 3 | 4 |
| 50 - 54 | 5 | 10 | 10 | 7 | 1 | 5 |
| 55 - 59 | 1 | 1 | 15 | 3 | 1 | 0 |
| 60 or over | 3 | 1 | 11 | 6 | 3 | 2 |

| People without age/sex data | 25 | | 28 | | 5 | |
| Total people | 362 | | 641 | | 203 | |
| Number of families | 96 | | 127 | | 83 | |

TABLE 2

Demographic Comparison of Interviewed Lao
to Health Department Figures

Male

| Officially Reported Age | Department of Health | Interviewed | Difference |
|---|---|---|---|
| 1 - 4 | 20 | 30 | + 10 |
| 5 - 9 | 18 | 26 | + 8 |
| 10 - 14 | 25 | 20 | - 5 |
| 15 - 19 | 15 | 16 | + 1 |
| 20 - 24 | 36 | 12 | - 24 |
| 25 - 29 | 15 | 9 | - 6 |
| 30 - 34 | 11 | 18 | + 7 |
| 35 - 39 | 14 | 11 | - 3 |
| 40 - 44 | 12 | 7 | - 5 |
| 45 - 49 | 2 | 2 | 0 |
| 50 - 54 | 10 | 3 | - 7 |
| 55 - 59 | 1 | 1 | 0 |
| 60 or over | 1 | 2 | + 1 |

TABLE 3

Demographic Comparison of Interviewed Lao
to Health Department Figures

Female

| Officially Reported Age | Department of Health | Interviewed | Difference |
|---|---|---|---|
| 1 - 4 | 13 | 23 | + 10 |
| 5 - 9 | 35 | 22 | - 13 |
| 10 - 14 | 18 | 18 | 0 |
| 15 - 19 | 19 | 5 | - 14 |
| 20 - 24 | 14 | 9 | - 5 |
| 25 - 29 | 17 | 20 | + 3 |
| 30 - 34 | 9 | 9 | 0 |
| 35 - 39 | 13 | 6 | - 7 |
| 40 - 44 | 4 | 5 | + 1 |
| 45 - 49 | 6 | 2 | - 4 |
| 50 - 54 | 5 | 1 | - 4 |
| 55 - 59 | 1 | 1 | 0 |
| 60 or over | 3 | 4 | + 1 |

As one can see, the figures do not match, particularly in the younger ages. One factor, previously mentioned, is that new births are not recorded in official records.

BIBLIOGRAPHY


Academy for Contemporary Problems
    1979    Human Systems: A Manual and Service Inventory
            for American Mental Health Practitioners and
            Indochinese Social Service Workers.  Columbus:
            Academy for Contemporary Problems.


Adams, Nina and Alfred McCoy (eds.)
    1970    Laos: War and Revolution.  New York:  Harper
            and Row, Publishers.


Andrianoff, David I.
    1979    "The Effect of the Laotian Conflict on Meo
            Ethnic Identity".  In Nationalism and the Crisis
            of Ethnic Minorities in Asia.  Jai S. Kang,
            ed. Westport, Conn:  Greenwood Press.


Bernard, William
    1976    "Immigrants and Refugees:  Their Similarities,
            Differences, and Needs."  International Migration
            Review 14:267-281.


Boone, Margaret S.
    1981    "Metropolitan Ethnography."     Anthropological
            Quarterly, Vol. 54, No. 2, pp 55-59.


Bourguignon, Erika
    1980    World of Women:  Anthropological Studies of
            Women in the Societies of the World.  New York:
            Praeger.


Branfman, Fred (ed.)
    1972    Voices from the Plain of Jars:    Life under
            an Air War.  New York:  Harper Colophon Books.


Burchett, Wilfred
    1970    The Second Indochina War:  Cambodia and Laos.
            New York:  International Publishers.


Burling, Robbins
    1965    Hill Farms and Padi Fields.  Englewood Cliffs,
            N.J.:  Prentice-Hall, Inc.

Chaplier, Georges and J. Van Malderghem
    1971    "Plain of Jars:  Social Changes under Five
            Years of Pathet Lao Administration." <u>Asia</u>
            <u>Quarterly</u> 1:63-89.

Cohen, Eugene N. and Edwin Eames
    1982    <u>Cultural Anthropology</u>.  Boston:  Little, Brown,
            and Company.

Condominas, Georges
    1975    "Phiban Cults in Rural Laos."  <u>In</u> Change and
            Persistence in Thai Society.  William Skinner
            and T.A. Kirsch, eds.  Ithaca: Cornell University
            Press.

Cooper, Robert G.
    1978    "Dynamic Tension:  Symbiosis and Contradiction
            in Hmong Social Relations."  <u>In</u> The New Economic
            Anthropology.  John Clammer, ed.  London:
            MacMillan Press.

    1979    "The Yao Jua Relationship:  Patterns of Affinal
            Alliance and Residence Among the Hmong of Northern
            Thailand."  <u>Ethnology</u> 28:173-181.

David, H.
    1969    "Involuntary International Migration."  <u>Inter-</u>
            <u>national Migration Review</u> 7.

Dundes, Alan (ed.)
    1965    <u>The Study of Forklore</u>.  Englewood Cliffs, N.J.:
            Prentice-Hall, Inc.

Dunnigan, Timothy
    1982    "Segmentary Kinship in an Urban Society:  the
            Hmong of St. Paul-Minneapolis."  <u>Anthropological</u>
            <u>Quarterly</u>, Vol. 55, No. 3, 1982, pp. 126-134.

Eisenstadt, S. N.
    1954    <u>The Absorption of Immigrants</u>.  Glencoe, Il:
            Free Press

Everingham, John
    1980    "One Family's Odyssey to America" <u>National</u>
            <u>Geographic</u>  157(5):642-661, May 1980.

Fall, Bernard
    1969    <u>Anatomy of a Crisis:  The Laotian Crisis of</u>
            <u>1960-1961</u>.  Garden City:  Doubleday and Co.,
            Inc.

Finnan, Christine
    1982    "Community Influence on the Occupational Adaption
            of Vietnamese Refugees." Anthropological Quarterly,
            Vol. 55, No. 3, July 1982, pp.146-160.

Garrett, W.E.
    1974    "No Place to Run:  The Hmong of Laos."  National
            Geographic 145(1):78-111, January 1974.

    1980    "Thailand:  Refuge from Terror."  National
            Geographic 157(5):633-642, May 1980.

Greenbaum, Leonora
    1973    "Possession Trance in Sub-Saharan Africa: A
            Descriptive Analysis of Fourteen Societies."
            In Religion, Altered States of Consciousness,
            and Social Change.  Erika Bourguignon, ed.
            Columbus:  Ohio State University Press.

Gordon, Milton M.
    1964    Assimilation in American Life:  The Role of
            Race, Religion, and National Origions.  New
            York:  Oxford University Press.

Gregory, James R.
    1984    "The Myth of the Male Ethnographer and the
            Woman's World".  American Anthropologist, Vol. 86,
            Number 2, pp. 316-327.

Gua, Bo
    1975    "Opium, Bombs, and Trees:  the Future of the
            Hmong Tribesmen in Nothern Thailand."  Journal
            of Contemporary Asia 5:70-81.

Haines, David
    1982    "Southeast Asian Refugees in the United States:
            the Interaction of Kinship and Public Policy."
            Antropological Quarterly Vol. 55, No. 3, July
            1982, pp. 170-181.

Haines, David, Dorothy Rutherford, and Patrick Thomas
    1981a   "Family and Community Among Vietnamese Refugees."
            International Migration Review.  Vol. 15, Numbers
            1-2, Spring-Summer 1981, pp. 310-319.

    1981b   "The Case for Exploratory Fieldwork: Understanding
            the Adjustment of Vietnamese Refugees in the
            Washington Area."  Anthropological Quarterly,
            Vol. 54, No. 2, pp 94-102.

Halpern, Barbara and Joel Halpern
    1964   "Laos and America -- A Retrospective View."
        South Atlantic Quarterly 63(2):175-187.

Halpern, Joel
    1963   "Traditional Medicine and the Role of Phi in
        Laos." The Eastern Anthropologist 16(3):191-200.

    1965   Govenment, Politics, and Social Structure in
        Laos. New Haven: Yale University, Southeast
        Asian Studies Monograph Series.

Hanks, Lucien M.
    1975   "The Thai Social Order as Entourage and Circle"
        In Change and Persistance in Thai Society.
        William Skinner and T.A. Kirsch (eds.) Ithaca:
        Cornell University Press

Honigman, John J.
    1976   The Development of Anthropological Ideas.
        Homewood, Il: The Dorsey Press.

Hoskins, Marilyn W.
    1976   "Vietnamese Women: Their Roles and Their Options"
        In Changing Identities in Modern Southeast
        Asia. David Banks, ed. the Hague: Mouton
        Publications.

Howell, David R.
    1982   "Refugee Resettlement and Public Policy: A
        Role for Anthropology". Anthropological Quarterly,
        Vol. 55, No. 3, July 1982, pp. 119-125.

Hull, Valerie L.
    1982   Women in Java's Rural Middle Class: Progress
        or Regress." In Women of Southeast Asia.
        Penny Van Esterik, ed. Center for Southeast
        Asian Studies, Occassional Paper Number 9,
        Northern Illinois University.

Huyck, Earl E. and Rona Fields
    1981   "Impact of Resettlement on Refugee Children."
        International Migration Review, Vol. 15, Numbers
        1-2, Spring-Summer, 1981, pp. 246-254.

Indochina Refugee Action Center
    1979   A Description and Directory of National Organi-
        zations and People Involved in Processing and
        Resettlement of Indochinese Refugees in America.
        Special Report, October 1979. Washington,
        D.C.: Indochina Refugee Action Center.

1980a    Indochinese Mutual Assistance Association.
         By Diana Bui. Washington, D.C.:    Indochina
         Refugee Action Center.

1980b    Statistical Update on Indochina Refugee Situation.
         April 15, 1980. Washington, D.C.:    Indochina
         Refugee Action Center.

1980c    Special Report: Physical and Emotional Health
         Care Needs of Indochinese Refugees.   March
         20, 1980. Compiled by Court Robinson. Washington,
         D.C.:   Indochina Refugee Action Center.

Indochinese Mental Health Project
    1980    Social/Cultural Customs:   Similarities and
            Differences between Vietnamese-Cambodians-H'mong-
            Lao. Minneapolis, Minnesota

Ingersoll, Jasper
    1966    "Fatalism in Village Thailand" Anthropological
            Quarterly, Vol. 39, July 1966, pp. 200-221

    1975    "Merit and Identity in Village Thailand" In
            Change and Persistence in Thai Society.   William
            Skinner and T.A. Kirsch, eds. Ithaca:    Cornell
            University Press.

Kales, David
    1970    "The Refugees of Laos."   The Nation, January
            26, 1970, pp. 76-77.

Keller, Stephen
    1975    Uprooting and Social Change: The Role of Refugees
            in Development.   Delhi:   Manohar Book Services.

Kelly, Gail
    1977    From Vietnam to America:   A Chronicle of the
            Vietnamese Immigration to the United States.
            Boulder:  Westview Press.

Kennedy, Edward
    1981    "Refugee Act of 1980."   International Migration
            Review, Vol. 15, Numbers 1-2, Spring-Summer
            1981, pp. 141-156.

Keyes, Charles F.
    1975    "Kin Groups in a Thai-Lao Community".   In Change
            and Persistence in Thai Society. William Skinner
            and T.A. Kirsch, eds. Ithaca:   Cornell University
            Press.

1977    The Golden Peninsula.    New York:   MacMillan
Press.

Kirsch, Thomas A.
    1984    "Buddhism, Sex-Roles and the Thai Economy."
        In Women of Southeast Asia.  Penny Van Esterick,
        ed. Center for Southeast Asian Studies, Occassional
        Paper No. 9, Northern Illinois University,
        pp. 16-41.

Kleinmann, Howard H. and James P. Daniel
    1981    "Indochinese Resettlement:  Language, Education
        and Social Services."  International Migration
        Review, Vol. 15, Numbers 1-2, Spring-Summer
        1981, pp. 239-245.

Kundstadter, Peter (ed.)
    1967    Southeast Asian Tribes, Minorities, and Nations.
        Princeton, N.J.:  Princeton University Press.

Kunz, Egon F.
    1973    "The Refugee in Flight:  Kinetic Models and
        Forms of Displacement."  International Migration
        Review, Vol. 7, Summer 1973.

    1981    "Exile and Resettlement:  Refugee Theory."
        International Migration Review, Vol. 15, Numbers
        1-2, Spring-Summer 1981, pp. 42-51.

Laderman, Carol C.
        "Putting Malay Women in Their Place"  In Women
        of Southeast Asia.  Penny Van Esterik, ed. Center
        for Southeast Asian Studies, Occassional Paper
        Number 9, Northern Illinois University.

Lasker, Gabriel W. and Robert N. Tyzzer
    1982    Physical Anthropology. New York:  Holt, Rinehart
        and Winston.

LeBar, Frank and Adrienne Suddard (eds.)
    1967    Laos:  Its People, Its Society, Its Culture.
        Third printing, revised.  New Haven:  HRAF
        Press.

LeBar, Frank, Gerald Hickey, and John Musgrave (eds.)
    1964    Ethnic Groups of Mainland Southeast Asia.
        New Haven:  HRAF Press.

Liu, William, Mary Anne Lamanna, and Alice Murata
    1979    Transition to Nowhere:  Vietnamese Refugees
        in America. Nashville:  Charter House.

Luong, Hy Van
    1984    "Analysis of Rules, Structural Contradictions
            and Meanings in Vietnamese Kinship". American
            Anthropologist, Vol. 86, Number 2, pp. 290-315.

Lyman, Thomas A.
    1968    "Green Miao (meo) Spirit Ceremonies." Ethnologica
            4:1-28.

Malinowski, Bronislaw
    1922    "On the Methods and Aims of Ethnographic
            Fieldwork". Reprint in Every Man His Way.
            Alan Dundes, ed. 1968. Englewood Cliffs, N.J.:
            Prentice-Hall.

Maloof, Patricia S.
    1981    "Fieldwork and the Folk Health Sector in the
            Washington, D.C. Metropolitan Area." Anthropo-
            logical Quarterly, Vol. 54, No. 2, pp 68-75

Messerschmidt, Donald (ed.)
    1981    Anthropology at Home in North America. Cambridge:
            Cambridge University Press.

Muecke, Marjorie A.
    1983    "Caring for Southeast Asian Refugee Patients
            in the USA." American Journal of Public Health,
            Vol. 73, No. 4, April 1983, pp. 431-438.

Murdock, George Peter (ed.)
    1960    Social Structure in Southeast Asia. Chicago:
            Quadrangle Books.

Murphy, H.B.M. (ed.)
    1955    Flight and Resettlement. Paris: UNESCO.

Mosel, James N.
    1966    "Fatalism in Thai Bureaucratic Decision-Making".
            Anthropological Quarterly, Vol. 39, July 1966,
            Number 3, pp. 191-199

Newman, William M.
    1973    American Pluralism. New York: Harper and
            Row.

Orbach, Michael and Janese Beckwith
    1982    "Indochinese Adaptation and Local Government
            Policy: An Example from Monterey." Anthropological
            Quarterly, Vol. 55, no. 3, July 1982, pp. 135-145.

Osborne, Milton
    1979    Southeast Asia:    An Introductory History.
            London:  George Allen and Unwin.

Peacock, James L. and A. Thomas Kirsch
    1980    The Human Direction.    Englewood Cliffs, N.J.:
            Prentice-Hall.

Phillips, H.P.
    1965    Thai Peasant Personality.  Los Angeles: University
            of California, Press.

Potter, Sulamith Heins
    1977    Family Life in a Northern Thai Village:  A
            Study in the Structural Significance of Women.
            Berkeley:  University of California, Press.

Scott, George
    1982    "The Hmong Refugee Community in San Diego:
            Theoretical and Practical Implications of its
            Continuing Ethnic Solidarity."  Anthropological
            Quarterly, Vol. 55, No. 3, July 1982, pp. 146-160.

Scudder, Thayer and Elizabeth Colson
    1982    "From Welfare to Development:  A Conceptual
            Framework for the Analysis of Dislocated People".
            In Involuntary Migration and Resettlement:
            The Problems and Responses of Dislocated People.
            Art Hansen and Anthony Oliver-Smith editors.
            Boulder:  Westview Press.

Shaplan, Robert
    1977    "A Reporter at Large:  Survivors."  The New
            Yorker.  September 7, 1977, pp. 33-66.

Smalley, William
    1956    "The Gospel and the Cultures of Laos."  Practical
            Anthropology 3(3):47-57.

Social Science Research Council Seminar
    1954    "Acculturation:  An Exploratory Formulation".
            American Anthropologist, Vol. 56, Number 6,
            pp. 973-1002.

Spiro, Melford E.
    1977    Kinship and Marriage in Burma:  A Cultural
            and Psychodynamic Analysis. Berkeley: University
            of California Press.

Stein, Barry
    1978    "Indochinese Refugees:  The New Boat People."
            Migration Today, Vol. 6, Number 5, December
            1978.

    1979    "Occupational Adjustment of Refugees:  The
            Vietnamese in the United States." International
            Migration Review, Vol. 13, No. 1, Spring 1979,
            pp. 22-45.

    1980    "The Refugee Experience:  An Overview of Refugee
            Research."  A paper presented at a conference
            on the Refugee Experience sponsored by the
            Royal Anthropological Institute and The Minority
            Rights Group.  London, England, February 22-24,
            1980.

    1981    "The Refugee Experience:  Defining the Parameters
            of a Field of Study." International Migration
            Review, Vol. 15, Numbers 1-2, Spring-Summer
            1981, pp. 320-330.

Stevenson, Charles
    1972    The End of Nowhere:  American Policy Towards
            Laos Since 1954.  Boston:  Beacon Press.

Thee, Marek
    1973    Notes of a Witness:  Laos and the Second Indochina
            War.  New York:  Random House.

Thomas, David Hurst
    1976    Figuring Anthropology:  First Principles of
            Probability and Statistics.  N.Y.:  Holt, Rinehart
            and Winston.

Van Amersfoort, Hans
    1982    Immigration and the Formation of Minority Groups.
            Cambridge:  Cambridge University Press.

Van Esterik, John
    1983    Untitled final report RFQ-48-82-HHS-0S.  "To
            provide an understanding of the individual,
            social, and cultural characteristics of adjustment
            and refugee program use of Laotian refugees."
            Received through correspondence.

Van Esterik, Penny
    1982    "Laywomen in Theravada Buddhism".  In Women
            of Southeast Asia.  Penny Van Esterik, ed.
            Center for Southeast Asian Studies, Occassional
            Paper number 9, Northern Illinois University,
            (Also see the Introduction.)

Westermeyer, Joseph
    1971    "Use of Alcohol and Opium by the Meo of Laos."
            American Journal of Psychiatry 127:59-63.

    1974    "Opium Smoking in Laos:  A Survey of 40 Addicts."
            Journal of Psychiatry 131:165-170.

Winkler, Elizabeth
    1981    "Voluntary Agencies and Government Policy."
            International Migration Review, Vol 15, Numbers
            1-2, Spring-Summer 1981, pp. 95-98.

The Wizard of Oz
    1939    director:  Victor Fleming.  Metro Goldwyn Meyer.

Wright, Robert
    1981    "Voluntary Agencies and the Resettlement of
            Refugees".  International Migration Review,
            Vol. 15, Numbers 1-2, Spring-Summer 1981, pp.
            157-174.

# INDEX

189